Editorial Project Manager
Eric Migliaccio

Editor in Chief
Brent L. Fox, M. Ed.

Creative Director
Sarah M. Fournier

Cover Artist
Diem Pascarella

Imaging
Amanda R. Harter

Publisher
Mary D. Smith, M.S. Ed.

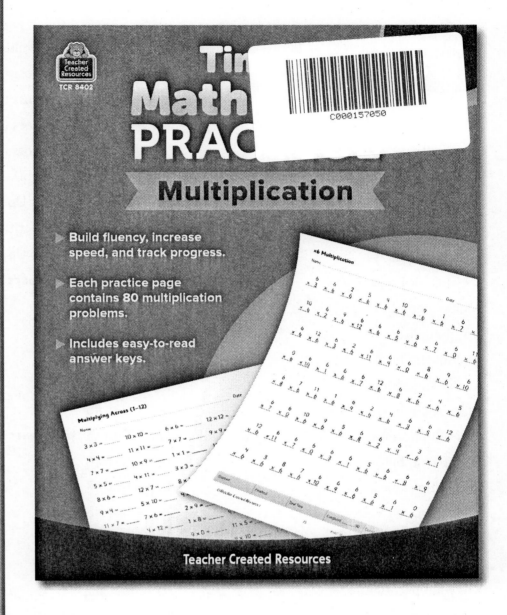

Teacher Created Resources
12621 Western Avenue
Garden Grove, CA 92841
www.teachercreated.com
ISBN: 978-1-4206-2144-0
©2021 Teacher Created Resources
Reprinted, 2023
Made in U.S.A.

Table of Contents

Introduction

This series of math practice books is designed to help students build confidence in their math abilities, and then bring that confidence into testing situations. As students develop fluency with math facts and operations, they improve their ability and flexibility in solving different types of math problems comfortably and quickly.

Each of the 48 practice pages in this book has 80 multiplication problems, giving students multiple opportunities to develop speed and fluency. Problems in this book are oriented in two different ways: up and down, left to right. Fluency is built systematically, first by multiplying numbers by 1, then by 2, then 3, and so on up to 12. Challenges are added slowly but surely, as new numbers and problems are introduced, combined, and rearranged. The book ends with 9 cumulative tests that offer students a mixture of multiplication facts that would typically be found in testing situations.

At the bottom of each page, you will find a section that can be used to record a student's progress. Use this to record any or all of the following: the time the student started, the time the student ended, the total time taken, how many problems out of 80 were completed, and how many were correctly answered.*

* Keep in mind that timing can sometimes add to the stress of learning. To establish a timing system, try following these steps:

1. Allow your student(s) to complete a few worksheets without officially timing them. This will give you a sense of how long your student(s) needs to complete a page.

2. Before you begin timing student(s), remind them that answers must be written legibly. Reinforce this rule often so that it is established before timing begins.

3. Once you have established how long it takes your student(s) to complete a page, ask them to take a timed test to see how it works. Adjust the time as needed.

4. Work to improve the number of correct answers within the given time. Remind your student(s) that being accurate is more important than being fast!

5. Encourage your learner(s) to try to do their best each time, to review their results, and to spend time working on areas where they had difficulties.

A tracking sheet is provided on page 4 of this book. Use the second column to record the number of problems the student answered correctly. The final column may be used for any purpose that helps you and your student(s) keep track of their progress. Here are some ideas:

• the score as a percent

• the date the test was taken

• your initials or the student's initials

Tracking Sheet

Name _____

Multiplying by 1		
page 5	/80	

Multiplying by 2		
page 6	/80	
page 7	/80	

Multiplying by 3		
page 8	/80	
page 9	/80	

Multiplying by 4		
page 10	/80	
page 11	/80	

Multiplying by 5		
page 12	/80	
page 13	/80	

Multiplying by 6		
page 14	/80	
page 15	/80	

Multiplying by 7		
page 16	/80	
page 17	/80	

Multiplying by 8		
page 18	/80	
page 19	/80	

Multiplying by 9		
page 20	/80	
page 21	/80	

Multiplying by 10		
page 22	/80	
page 23	/80	

Multiplying by 11		
page 24	/80	
page 25	/80	

Multiplying by 12		
page 26	/80	
page 27	/80	

Multiplying by 1–3		
page 28	/80	
page 29	/80	

Multiplying by 4–6		
page 30	/80	
page 31	/80	

Multiplying by 7–9		
page 32	/80	
page 33	/80	

Multiplying by 10–12		
page 34	/80	
page 35	/80	

Multiplying Across		
page 36	/80	
page 37	/80	
page 38	/80	
page 39	/80	

Answers Up to 50		
page 40	/80	
page 41	/80	

Answers Up to 100		
page 42	/80	
page 43	/80	

Cumulative Tests		
page 44	/80	
page 45	/80	
page 46	/80	
page 47	/80	
page 48	/80	
page 49	/80	
page 50	/80	
page 51	/80	
page 52	/80	

Multiplying by 1

Name _____   Date _____

0 × 1	10 × 1	12 × 1	9 × 1	11 × 1	8 × 1	5 × 1	6 × 1	7 × 1	4 × 1
5 × 1	12 × 1	9 × 1	3 × 1	7 × 1	4 × 1	8 × 1	2 × 1	0 × 1	11 × 1
4 × 1	6 × 1	3 × 1	0 × 1	8 × 1	7 × 1	12 × 1	5 × 1	9 × 1	1 × 1
3 × 1	0 × 1	1 × 1	8 × 1	2 × 1	5 × 1	6 × 1	9 × 1	10 × 1	7 × 1
2 × 1	8 × 1	0 × 1	4 × 1	3 × 1	6 × 1	1 × 1	7 × 1	5 × 1	9 × 1
8 × 1	7 × 1	6 × 1	2 × 1	4 × 1	1 × 1	10 × 1	11 × 1	3 × 1	5 × 1
1 × 1	2 × 1	7 × 1	5 × 1	6 × 1	9 × 1	0 × 1	4 × 1	8 × 1	3 × 1
9 × 1	4 × 1	10 × 1	6 × 1	5 × 1	2 × 1	7 × 1	3 × 1	1 × 1	12 × 1

Started:	Finished:	Total Time:	Completed: _____ /80	Correct: _____ /80

Multiplying by 2

Name _____   Date _____

2 × 2	3 × 2	10 × 2	4 × 2	6 × 2	5 × 2	0 × 2	9 × 2	7 × 2	1 × 2
4 × 2	8 × 2	1 × 2	9 × 2	7 × 2	11 × 2	9 × 2	5 × 2	12 × 2	2 × 2
0 × 2	10 × 2	3 × 2	5 × 2	4 × 2	12 × 2	5 × 2	6 × 2	8 × 2	7 × 2
1 × 2	5 × 2	7 × 2	6 × 2	0 × 2	8 × 2	6 × 2	3 × 2	2 × 2	4 × 2
5 × 2	0 × 2	8 × 2	1 × 2	2 × 2	7 × 2	11 × 2	4 × 2	9 × 2	6 × 2
6 × 2	1 × 2	5 × 2	2 × 2	11 × 2	4 × 2	12 × 2	1 × 2	0 × 2	9 × 2
3 × 2	2 × 2	6 × 2	7 × 2	8 × 2	10 × 2	7 × 2	12 × 2	5 × 2	11 × 2
9 × 2	6 × 2	4 × 2	8 × 2	5 × 2	2 × 2	8 × 2	7 × 2	10 × 2	12 × 2

Started:	Finished:	Total Time:	Completed: _____ /80	Correct: _____ /80

×2 Multiplication

Name _____   Date _____

2 × 2	5 × 2	2 × 0	2 × 7	4 × 2	2 × 12	6 × 2	2 × 1	2 × 11	3 × 2
2 × 1	2 × 3	2 × 6	2 × 11	5 × 2	2 × 10	2 × 2	2 × 7	2 × 8	9 × 2
7 × 2	2 × 9	2 × 1	2 × 3	2 × 8	2 × 2	2 × 5	2 × 6	2 × 0	5 × 2
4 × 2	2 × 8	5 × 2	8 × 2	2 × 1	2 × 7	2 × 9	3 × 2	2 × 2	2 × 0
2 × 6	11 × 2	2 × 2	2 × 5	7 × 2	2 × 3	2 × 8	9 × 2	12 × 2	2 × 4
10 × 2	2 × 7	7 × 2	6 × 2	3 × 2	5 × 2	1 × 2	0 × 2	4 × 2	2 × 2
2 × 5	6 × 2	2 × 9	1 × 2	2 × 2	4 × 2	10 × 2	5 × 2	2 × 3	2 × 8
2 × 12	2 × 4	3 × 2	2 × 2	2 × 6	9 × 2	7 × 2	8 × 2	2 × 5	2 × 1

Started:	Finished:	Total Time:	Completed: _____ /80	Correct: _____ /80

Multiplying by 3

Name _____   Date _____

1 × 3	4 × 3	3 × 3	2 × 3	7 × 3	6 × 3	0 × 3	5 × 3	8 × 3	10 × 3
7 × 3	9 × 3	1 × 3	10 × 3	0 × 3	12 × 3	5 × 3	11 × 3	4 × 3	3 × 3
8 × 3	10 × 3	6 × 3	3 × 3	9 × 3	5 × 3	4 × 3	2 × 3	7 × 3	0 × 3
2 × 3	7 × 3	10 × 3	12 × 3	4 × 3	9 × 3	3 × 3	6 × 3	5 × 3	8 × 3
3 × 3	12 × 3	8 × 3	11 × 3	5 × 3	7 × 3	10 × 3	1 × 3	6 × 3	4 × 3
4 × 3	5 × 3	11 × 3	6 × 3	3 × 3	0 × 3	8 × 3	9 × 3	1 × 3	2 × 3
6 × 3	3 × 3	2 × 3	7 × 3	10 × 3	4 × 3	1 × 3	0 × 3	9 × 3	5 × 3
11 × 3	2 × 3	4 × 3	8 × 3	1 × 3	3 × 3	9 × 3	7 × 3	0 × 3	12 × 3

Started:	Finished:	Total Time:	Completed: _____ /80	Correct: _____ /80

×3 Multiplication

Name _____   Date _____

3 × 3	3 × 6	2 × 3	5 × 3	4 × 3	0 × 3	9 × 3	1 × 3	3 × 7	12 × 3
3 × 12	3 × 2	9 × 3	3 × 8	6 × 3	3 × 5	3 × 3	7 × 3	3 × 0	11 × 3
6 × 3	5 × 3	3 × 10	2 × 3	3 × 1	3 × 4	3 × 0	8 × 3	9 × 3	3 × 7
10 × 3	3 × 9	3 × 1	3 × 6	3 × 7	12 × 3	3 × 8	2 × 3	4 × 3	5 × 3
3 × 8	12 × 3	0 × 3	10 × 3	3 × 9	2 × 3	4 × 3	3 × 11	3 × 5	6 × 3
3 × 7	3 × 8	6 × 3	9 × 3	11 × 3	10 × 3	2 × 3	4 × 3	3 × 3	3 × 1
2 × 3	3 × 4	3 × 7	3 × 0	3 × 12	3 × 1	5 × 3	3 × 10	3 × 8	3 × 9
4 × 3	3 × 3	8 × 3	7 × 3	3 × 2	3 × 9	3 × 6	5 × 3	3 × 11	0 × 3

Started:	Finished:	Total Time:	Completed: _____ /80	Correct: _____ /80

Multiplying by 4

Name _____ Date _____

10 × 4	4 × 4	3 × 4	9 × 4	1 × 4	0 × 4	2 × 4	8 × 4	7 × 4	5 × 4
2 × 4	12 × 4	1 × 4	11 × 4	7 × 4	5 × 4	9 × 4	4 × 4	0 × 4	12 × 4
5 × 4	1 × 4	6 × 4	0 × 4	8 × 4	4 × 4	10 × 4	7 × 4	11 × 4	2 × 4
9 × 4	7 × 4	10 × 4	8 × 4	2 × 4	3 × 4	1 × 4	5 × 4	12 × 4	6 × 4
7 × 4	9 × 4	8 × 4	4 × 4	3 × 4	2 × 4	0 × 4	11 × 4	5 × 4	10 × 4
0 × 4	5 × 4	7 × 4	12 × 4	4 × 4	8 × 4	6 × 4	1 × 4	3 × 4	9 × 4
12 × 4	3 × 4	2 × 4	5 × 4	6 × 4	1 × 4	7 × 4	9 × 4	8 × 4	11 × 4
11 × 4	2 × 4	4 × 4	10 × 4	5 × 4	9 × 4	8 × 4	0 × 4	1 × 4	7 × 4

Started: _____ Finished: _____ Total Time: _____ Completed: _____/80 Correct: _____/80

×4 Multiplication

Name _____ Date _____

4	4	2	5	4	12	9	1	4	8
× 3	× 6	× 4	× 4	× 4	× 4	× 4	× 4	× 7	× 4

4	4	9	4	12	4	3	7	4	11
× 10	× 2	× 4	× 8	× 4	× 5	× 4	× 4	× 0	× 4

6	5	4	2	4	4	4	8	11	4
× 4	× 4	× 3	× 4	× 1	× 4	× 0	× 4	× 4	× 7

0	4	4	4	4	3	4	2	4	5
× 4	× 9	× 12	× 6	× 7	× 4	× 8	× 4	× 4	× 4

4	7	0	1	4	2	4	4	4	6
× 11	× 4	× 4	× 4	× 9	× 4	× 12	× 3	× 5	× 4

4	4	6	9	11	10	2	4	12	4
× 7	× 10	× 4	× 4	× 4	× 4	× 4	× 4	× 4	× 1

2	4	4	4	4	4	10	6	4	4
× 4	× 4	× 7	× 0	× 3	× 1	× 4	× 4	× 8	× 9

4	3	8	11	4	4	4	5	4	12
× 4	× 4	× 4	× 4	× 2	× 9	× 6	× 4	× 1	× 4

Started:	Finished:	Total Time:	Completed: _____ /80	Correct: _____ /80

Multiplying by 5

Name _____   Date _____

2	5	1	3	10	9	4	12	0	8
× 5	× 5	× 5	× 5	× 5	× 5	× 5	× 5	× 5	× 5
4	0	6	11	12	10	9	3	1	2
× 5	× 5	× 5	× 5	× 5	× 5	× 5	× 5	× 5	× 5
10	1	2	9	11	6	5	8	3	7
× 5	× 5	× 5	× 5	× 5	× 5	× 5	× 5	× 5	× 5
11	10	9	5	0	3	6	2	7	4
× 5	× 5	× 5	× 5	× 5	× 5	× 5	× 5	× 5	× 5
5	7	3	0	2	4	1	9	8	12
× 5	× 5	× 5	× 5	× 5	× 5	× 5	× 5	× 5	× 5
6	11	12	1	3	8	2	0	5	10
× 5	× 5	× 5	× 5	× 5	× 5	× 5	× 5	× 5	× 5
3	9	4	2	8	1	7	5	6	0
× 5	× 5	× 5	× 5	× 5	× 5	× 5	× 5	× 5	× 5
9	12	0	6	5	7	8	10	4	11
× 5	× 5	× 5	× 5	× 5	× 5	× 5	× 5	× 5	× 5

Started:	Finished:	Total Time:	Completed: _____ /80	Correct: _____ /80

×5 Multiplication

Name _____ Date _____

1 × 5	5 × 7	3 × 5	5 × 2	5 × 8	6 × 5	12 × 5	9 × 5	5 × 5	4 × 5
7 × 5	5 × 10	5 × 1	9 × 5	4 × 5	5 × 2	5 × 5	11 × 5	8 × 5	6 × 5
5 × 8	9 × 5	11 × 5	5 × 3	10 × 5	5 × 5	5 × 4	5 × 0	2 × 5	5 × 1
5 × 12	4 × 5	0 × 5	1 × 5	5 × 5	10 × 5	5 × 3	5 × 8	6 × 5	5 × 11
3 × 5	5 × 5	5 × 10	5 × 12	5 × 6	7 × 5	2 × 5	4 × 5	1 × 5	5 × 9
11 × 5	5 × 3	5 × 7	6 × 5	5 × 1	5 × 0	8 × 5	2 × 5	9 × 5	10 × 5
5 × 6	5 × 8	2 × 5	5 × 7	5 × 9	5 × 11	5 × 1	5 × 5	5 × 0	12 × 5
5 × 5	11 × 5	4 × 5	8 × 5	0 × 5	12 × 5	5 × 9	5 × 10	7 × 5	5 × 2

Started:	Finished:	Total Time:	Completed: _____ /80	Correct: _____ /80

Multiplying by 6

Name _____ Date _____

4 × 6	5 × 6	1 × 6	2 × 6	3 × 6	10 × 6	0 × 6	8 × 6	7 × 6	6 × 6
6 × 6	11 × 6	7 × 6	9 × 6	12 × 6	3 × 6	5 × 6	4 × 6	0 × 6	2 × 6
10 × 6	12 × 6	8 × 6	11 × 6	6 × 6	0 × 6	4 × 6	7 × 6	9 × 6	5 × 6
7 × 6	6 × 6	2 × 6	1 × 6	10 × 6	8 × 6	3 × 6	5 × 6	4 × 6	9 × 6
9 × 6	1 × 6	10 × 6	12 × 6	8 × 6	11 × 6	2 × 6	6 × 6	5 × 6	7 × 6
12 × 6	10 × 6	4 × 6	6 × 6	7 × 6	2 × 6	8 × 6	1 × 6	3 × 6	0 × 6
3 × 6	0 × 6	11 × 6	7 × 6	2 × 6	5 × 6	1 × 6	9 × 6	8 × 6	12 × 6
2 × 6	7 × 6	5 × 6	8 × 6	4 × 6	6 × 6	9 × 6	10 × 6	1 × 6	11 × 6

Started: _____ Finished: _____ Total Time: _____ Completed: _____ /80 Correct: _____ /80

×6 Multiplication

Name _____   Date _____

6 × 3	6 × 6	2 × 6	5 × 6	4 × 6	10 × 6	9 × 6	1 × 6	6 × 7	8 × 6
10 × 6	6 × 2	9 × 6	6 × 12	6 × 6	6 × 5	3 × 6	6 × 7	6 × 0	11 × 6
6 × 6	12 × 6	6 × 3	2 × 6	6 × 11	6 × 4	6 × 0	8 × 6	9 × 6	6 × 10
0 × 6	6 × 10	6 × 1	6 × 6	6 × 7	12 × 6	6 × 8	2 × 6	4 × 6	5 × 6
6 × 8	7 × 6	11 × 6	1 × 6	6 × 9	2 × 6	4 × 6	6 × 3	6 × 5	12 × 6
6 × 7	6 × 0	10 × 6	9 × 6	5 × 6	6 × 8	6 × 2	6 × 4	3 × 6	6 × 1
12 × 6	6 × 11	6 × 7	6 × 0	6 × 3	6 × 1	5 × 6	6 × 6	6 × 8	6 × 9
4 × 6	3 × 6	8 × 6	7 × 6	6 × 10	6 × 9	6 × 6	5 × 6	6 × 1	0 × 6

Started:	Finished:	Total Time:	Completed: _____ /80	Correct: _____ /80

Multiplying by 7

Name _____   Date _____

0	8	2	4	7	10	3	6	9	5
× 7	× 7	× 7	× 7	× 7	× 7	× 7	× 7	× 7	× 7

10	2	4	9	3	6	11	7	5	12
× 7	× 7	× 7	× 7	× 7	× 7	× 7	× 7	× 7	× 7

3	7	10	5	8	2	9	4	6	11
× 7	× 7	× 7	× 7	× 7	× 7	× 7	× 7	× 7	× 7

7	4	1	11	12	9	5	0	3	10
× 7	× 7	× 7	× 7	× 7	× 7	× 7	× 7	× 7	× 7

8	12	5	1	9	3	0	2	11	7
× 7	× 7	× 7	× 7	× 7	× 7	× 7	× 7	× 7	× 7

5	10	6	2	11	7	1	3	8	4
× 7	× 7	× 7	× 7	× 7	× 7	× 7	× 7	× 7	× 7

6	0	3	7	5	4	2	8	1	9
× 7	× 7	× 7	× 7	× 7	× 7	× 7	× 7	× 7	× 7

12	3	9	8	1	0	6	11	10	2
× 7	× 7	× 7	× 7	× 7	× 7	× 7	× 7	× 7	× 7

Started:	Finished:	Total Time:	Completed: _____ /80	Correct: _____ /80

×7 Multiplication

Name _____ Date _____

3 × 7	7 × 2	4 × 7	7 × 7	9 × 7	5 × 7	6 × 7	10 × 7	7 × 11	1 × 7
10 × 7	9 × 7	6 × 7	7 × 0	3 × 7	8 × 7	7 × 12	5 × 7	4 × 7	7 × 7
7 × 12	7 × 3	7 × 1	10 × 7	7 × 0	7 × 2	7 × 5	7 × 4	7 × 7	7 × 8
0 × 7	11 × 7	12 × 7	7 × 4	7 × 8	6 × 7	9 × 7	7 × 10	7 × 5	7 × 2
7 × 8	7 × 10	7 × 9	5 × 7	4 × 7	1 × 7	7 × 7	2 × 7	7 × 6	3 × 7
7 × 7	6 × 7	5 × 7	7 × 11	11 × 7	7 × 9	7 × 0	8 × 7	7 × 1	12 × 7
2 × 7	7 × 7	3 × 7	7 × 8	7 × 12	7 × 0	7 × 4	7 × 1	9 × 7	7 × 6
7 × 11	8 × 7	7 × 2	12 × 7	7 × 6	7 × 7	3 × 7	7 × 9	0 × 7	7 × 10

Started:	Finished:	Total Time:	Completed: _____ /80	Correct: _____ /80

Multiplying by 8

Name _____ Date _____

10	8	7	1	2	4	5	3	9	6
× 8	× 8	× 8	× 8	× 8	× 8	× 8	× 8	× 8	× 8

5	12	0	7	10	6	11	1	3	2
× 8	× 8	× 8	× 8	× 8	× 8	× 8	× 8	× 8	× 8

4	11	9	8	3	1	2	6	12	5
× 8	× 8	× 8	× 8	× 8	× 8	× 8	× 8	× 8	× 8

3	5	4	12	1	7	6	0	8	9
× 8	× 8	× 8	× 8	× 8	× 8	× 8	× 8	× 8	× 8

2	6	5	3	0	9	1	10	11	7
× 8	× 8	× 8	× 8	× 8	× 8	× 8	× 8	× 8	× 8

8	0	3	4	6	12	9	7	2	10
× 8	× 8	× 8	× 8	× 8	× 8	× 8	× 8	× 8	× 8

1	9	8	10	11	3	0	2	5	4
× 8	× 8	× 8	× 8	× 8	× 8	× 8	× 8	× 8	× 8

12	10	11	5	8	2	7	4	6	3
× 8	× 8	× 8	× 8	× 8	× 8	× 8	× 8	× 8	× 8

Started:	Finished:	Total Time:	Completed: _____ /80	Correct: _____ /80

×8 Multiplication

Name _____   Date _____

2 × 8	8 × 0	8 × 10	1 × 8	8 × 3	6 × 8	8 × 7	8 × 8	4 × 8	5 × 8
9 × 8	8 × 5	3 × 8	8 × 7	10 × 8	8 × 2	8 × 12	4 × 8	8 × 6	8 × 11
8 × 3	8 × 4	8 × 0	8 × 8	8 × 11	12 × 8	9 × 8	8 × 7	10 × 8	2 × 8
8 × 1	3 × 8	8 × 12	2 × 8	0 × 8	8 × 9	4 × 8	5 × 8	8 × 7	8 × 6
10 × 8	2 × 8	4 × 8	8 × 3	8 × 8	7 × 8	8 × 5	8 × 12	8 × 9	1 × 8
6 × 8	8 × 8	8 × 2	8 × 10	8 × 7	8 × 11	3 × 8	8 × 1	5 × 8	9 × 8
8 × 12	8 × 1	5 × 8	6 × 8	2 × 8	8 × 4	10 × 8	8 × 9	11 × 8	8 × 0
8 × 8	8 × 11	8 × 6	5 × 8	4 × 8	3 × 8	8 × 1	0 × 8	8 × 2	7 × 8

Started:	Finished:	Total Time:	Completed: _____ /80	Correct: _____ /80

Multiplying by 9

Name _____   Date _____

1	2	10	5	3	6	9	4	7	8
× 9	× 9	× 9	× 9	× 9	× 9	× 9	× 9	× 9	× 9

6	11	1	0	8	7	5	10	12	2
× 9	× 9	× 9	× 9	× 9	× 9	× 9	× 9	× 9	× 9

2	0	3	1	9	4	6	5	8	7
× 9	× 9	× 9	× 9	× 9	× 9	× 9	× 9	× 9	× 9

10	12	7	8	5	0	3	11	2	4
× 9	× 9	× 9	× 9	× 9	× 9	× 9	× 9	× 9	× 9

3	5	11	10	0	2	12	1	9	6
× 9	× 9	× 9	× 9	× 9	× 9	× 9	× 9	× 9	× 9

7	6	5	4	1	10	8	2	0	9
× 9	× 9	× 9	× 9	× 9	× 9	× 9	× 9	× 9	× 9

4	3	6	9	12	8	1	7	11	10
× 9	× 9	× 9	× 9	× 9	× 9	× 9	× 9	× 9	× 9

12	9	4	2	6	5	7	8	1	3
× 9	× 9	× 9	× 9	× 9	× 9	× 9	× 9	× 9	× 9

Started:	Finished:	Total Time:	Completed: _____ /80	Correct: _____ /80

×9 Multiplication

Name _____ Date _____

6 × 9	1 × 9	10 × 9	3 × 9	9 × 2	9 × 8	9 × 9	9 × 5	4 × 9	9 × 7
9 × 2	7 × 9	5 × 9	9 × 10	9 × 9	11 × 9	3 × 9	12 × 9	9 × 6	9 × 0
9 × 5	9 × 8	9 × 4	6 × 9	9 × 11	12 × 9	9 × 0	2 × 9	9 × 1	9 × 9
12 × 9	9 × 10	9 × 3	0 × 9	1 × 9	9 × 5	9 × 8	11 × 9	9 × 7	4 × 9
7 × 9	3 × 9	2 × 9	9 × 8	9 × 0	9 × 6	4 × 9	9 × 10	12 × 9	11 × 9
9 × 10	11 × 9	8 × 9	9 × 7	9 × 6	9 × 1	2 × 9	9 × 9	5 × 9	9 × 3
9 × 4	9 × 6	9 × 1	2 × 9	9 × 7	9 × 9	9 × 5	9 × 0	3 × 9	9 × 12
11 × 9	9 × 5	9 × 9	4 × 9	12 × 9	0 × 9	9 × 9	7 × 6	9 × 10	1 × 9

Started:	Finished:	Total Time:	Completed: _____ /80	Correct: _____ /80

Multiplying by 10

Name _____   Date _____

5 × 10	11 × 10	3 × 10	1 × 10	2 × 10	10 × 10	8 × 10	7 × 10	12 × 10	4 × 10
12 × 10	2 × 10	10 × 10	7 × 10	9 × 10	5 × 10	4 × 10	0 × 10	3 × 10	6 × 10
2 × 10	5 × 10	6 × 10	8 × 10	3 × 10	11 × 10	12 × 10	9 × 10	0 × 10	1 × 10
6 × 10	9 × 10	0 × 10	2 × 10	10 × 10	3 × 10	11 × 10	4 × 10	8 × 10	7 × 10
1 × 10	12 × 10	8 × 10	3 × 10	0 × 10	2 × 10	6 × 10	5 × 10	4 × 10	9 × 10
9 × 10	0 × 10	7 × 10	4 × 10	6 × 10	8 × 10	1 × 10	3 × 10	10 × 10	11 × 10
10 × 10	4 × 10	2 × 10	11 × 10	7 × 10	1 × 10	9 × 10	12 × 10	5 × 10	3 × 10
7 × 10	11 × 10	4 × 10	5 × 10	8 × 10	12 × 10	0 × 10	1 × 10	6 × 10	10 × 10

Started:	Finished:	Total Time:	Completed: _____ /80	Correct: _____ /80

×10 Multiplication

Name _____   Date _____

5	12	1	10	0	8	10	10	10	11
× 10	× 10	× 10	× 7	× 10	× 10	× 3	× 6	× 10	× 10
10	11	10	10	10	4	1	10	9	10
× 8	× 10	× 12	× 0	× 5	× 10	× 10	× 2	× 10	× 6
11	10	8	9	10	10	10	5	10	10
× 10	× 10	× 10	× 10	× 4	× 7	× 2	× 10	× 3	× 1
10	6	2	4	3	5	0	10	10	10
× 12	× 10	× 10	× 10	× 10	× 10	× 10	× 9	× 1	× 7
1	4	10	10	11	10	10	7	10	10
× 10	× 10	× 3	× 2	× 10	× 6	× 8	× 10	× 10	× 12
9	10	10	3	10	10	10	10	6	5
× 10	× 2	× 4	× 10	× 12	× 10	× 7	× 0	× 10	× 10
10	5	6	10	10	10	2	10	10	10
× 0	× 10	× 10	× 8	× 10	× 9	× 10	× 4	× 7	× 11
7	6	5	10	10	0	11	3	12	10
× 10	× 10	× 10	× 1	× 9	× 10	× 10	× 10	× 10	× 10

Started:	Finished:	Total Time:	Completed: _____ /80	Correct: _____ /80

Multiplying by 11

Name _____   Date _____

2 × 11	1 × 11	5 × 11	7 × 11	8 × 11	12 × 11	9 × 11	1 × 11	3 × 11	10 × 11
1 × 11	10 × 11	4 × 11	2 × 11	3 × 11	5 × 11	6 × 11	11 × 11	7 × 11	9 × 11
4 × 11	6 × 11	3 × 11	9 × 11	5 × 11	7 × 11	11 × 11	0 × 11	12 × 11	8 × 11
3 × 11	8 × 11	11 × 11	0 × 11	10 × 11	9 × 11	12 × 11	7 × 11	6 × 11	2 × 11
5 × 11	9 × 11	10 × 11	4 × 11	12 × 11	1 × 11	2 × 11	3 × 11	11 × 11	6 × 11
6 × 11	2 × 11	7 × 11	3 × 11	11 × 11	10 × 11	8 × 11	9 × 11	4 × 11	1 × 11
7 × 11	11 × 11	8 × 11	1 × 11	9 × 11	0 × 11	10 × 11	1 × 11	5 × 11	12 × 11
8 × 11	3 × 11	6 × 11	5 × 11	2 × 11	4 × 11	1 × 11	12 × 11	0 × 11	7 × 11

Started:	Finished:	Total Time:	Completed: _____ /80	Correct: _____ /80

×11 Multiplication

Name _____ Date _____

1	8	12	10	11	7	11	9	11	2
× 11	× 11	× 11	× 11	× 5	× 11	× 4	× 11	× 3	× 11
10	11	5	9	4	11	1	11	11	11
× 11	× 3	× 11	× 11	× 11	× 2	× 11	× 6	× 7	× 11
11	5	11	11	11	9	0	11	10	4
× 6	× 11	× 7	× 8	× 3	× 11	× 11	× 11	× 11	× 11
11	11	9	2	11	11	7	11	6	11
× 8	× 10	× 11	× 11	× 11	× 0	× 11	× 12	× 11	× 3
9	12	11	11	10	4	3	2	11	11
× 11	× 11	× 1	× 6	× 11	× 11	× 11	× 11	× 11	× 5
11	11	8	1	11	11	11	11	11	11
× 2	× 11	× 11	× 11	× 7	× 3	× 9	× 5	× 4	× 6
11	11	11	12	11	1	11	10	5	7
× 11	× 9	× 0	× 11	× 8	× 11	× 1	× 11	× 11	× 11
3	2	11	7	6	5	12	1	0	11
× 11	× 11	× 4	× 11	× 11	× 11	× 11	× 11	× 11	× 8

Started:	Finished:	Total Time:	Completed: _____ /80	Correct: _____ /80

Multiplying by 12

Name _____   Date _____

0 × 12	3 × 12	12 × 12	7 × 12	1 × 12	2 × 12	4 × 12	5 × 12	12 × 12	9 × 12
6 × 12	1 × 12	8 × 12	0 × 12	5 × 12	9 × 12	7 × 12	4 × 12	10 × 12	11 × 12
1 × 12	7 × 12	3 × 12	4 × 12	9 × 12	11 × 12	8 × 12	2 × 12	5 × 12	10 × 12
4 × 12	2 × 12	6 × 12	8 × 12	7 × 12	3 × 12	10 × 12	12 × 12	0 × 12	5 × 12
2 × 12	10 × 12	5 × 12	6 × 12	11 × 12	12 × 12	1 × 12	9 × 12	3 × 12	0 × 12
9 × 12	11 × 12	0 × 12	3 × 12	8 × 12	6 × 12	12 × 12	10 × 12	1 × 12	4 × 12
7 × 12	5 × 12	4 × 12	1 × 12	3 × 12	0 × 12	6 × 12	11 × 12	8 × 12	2 × 12
3 × 12	8 × 12	9 × 12	2 × 12	10 × 12	4 × 12	5 × 12	6 × 12	7 × 12	12 × 12

Started: _____ | Finished: _____ | Total Time: _____ | Completed: _____/80 | Correct: _____/80

×12 Multiplication

Name _____   Date _____

3 × 12	12 × 6	5 × 12	12 × 10	1 × 12	12 × 4	8 × 12	12 × 7	2 × 12	12 × 9
12 × 5	11 × 12	12 × 0	7 × 12	12 × 3	1 × 12	12 × 9	10 × 12	12 × 4	6 × 12
8 × 12	12 × 10	6 × 12	12 × 9	7 × 12	12 × 11	5 × 12	12 × 0	1 × 12	12 × 12
12 × 2	4 × 12	12 × 3	12 × 12	12 × 10	5 × 12	12 × 11	6 × 12	12 × 0	7 × 12
6 × 12	12 × 9	7 × 12	12 × 1	4 × 12	12 × 8	10 × 12	12 × 2	12 × 12	12 × 3
12 × 7	11 × 12	12 × 9	5 × 12	12 × 0	6 × 12	12 × 3	4 × 12	12 × 10	8 × 12
0 × 12	12 × 3	4 × 12	12 × 6	9 × 12	12 × 7	1 × 12	12 × 3	11 × 12	12 × 10
12 × 1	2 × 12	12 × 8	11 × 12	12 × 5	10 × 12	12 × 4	5 × 12	12 × 8	4 × 12

Started:	Finished:	Total Time:	Completed: _____/80	Correct: _____/80

Multiplying by 1s, 2s, and 3s

Name _____   Date _____

5	2	11	8	6	9	0	7	11	8
× 2	× 3	× 1	× 3	× 1	× 1	× 3	× 2	× 3	× 2

10	4	12	8	7	5	9	3	1	4
× 1	× 2	× 3	× 1	× 2	× 3	× 2	× 1	× 3	× 3

1	12	2	9	4	6	5	8	3	7
× 3	× 1	× 2	× 2	× 3	× 2	× 1	× 3	× 2	× 2

8	1	9	5	0	3	6	2	7	12
× 1	× 2	× 3	× 1	× 2	× 3	× 3	× 2	× 2	× 3

7	5	3	0	2	4	10	11	8	6
× 2	× 3	× 1	× 3	× 1	× 1	× 2	× 1	× 1	× 1

4	6	10	1	3	8	12	0	5	9
× 1	× 2	× 3	× 1	× 3	× 3	× 1	× 3	× 1	× 2

9	3	4	12	8	11	7	5	12	10
× 3	× 1	× 2	× 2	× 1	× 2	× 2	× 2	× 3	× 1

2	11	0	6	5	7	8	9	4	3
× 1	× 3	× 3	× 1	× 2	× 3	× 3	× 3	× 2	× 3

Started:	Finished:	Total Time:	Completed: _____ /80	Correct: _____ /80

×1, ×2, ×3 Multiplication

Name _____ Date _____

2 × 5	4 × 3	3 × 6	1 × 12	2 × 11	1 × 12	9 × 3	1 × 10	7 × 1	8 × 1
5 × 1	6 × 2	9 × 3	3 × 11	6 × 2	10 × 3	3 × 6	3 × 7	6 × 3	4 × 2
3 × 6	2 × 5	5 × 1	2 × 10	8 × 3	2 × 4	2 × 0	8 × 2	9 × 2	3 × 12
1 × 5	2 × 9	6 × 2	5 × 3	11 × 1	3 × 6	1 × 12	2 × 9	2 × 10	2 × 6
6 × 2	7 × 3	2 × 5	1 × 4	2 × 9	2 × 7	4 × 3	10 × 3	9 × 3	6 × 3
3 × 7	6 × 1	1 × 11	3 × 6	3 × 0	7 × 1	6 × 2	2 × 11	3 × 6	3 × 11
2 × 5	2 × 4	10 × 3	6 × 2	3 × 9	12 × 1	2 × 5	1 × 4	0 × 1	5 × 1
11 × 1	3 × 3	12 × 2	11 × 3	12 × 3	2 × 9	6 × 1	5 × 2	2 × 11	0 × 3

Started:	Finished:	Total Time:	Completed: _____ /80	Correct: _____ /80

Multiplying by 4s, 5s, and 6s

Name _____ Date _____

3 × 5	10 × 5	8 × 4	3 × 6	11 × 6	1 × 4	12 × 4	7 × 5	6 × 4	3 × 5
11 × 4	5 × 6	9 × 5	10 × 4	5 × 5	0 × 6	11 × 5	8 × 4	10 × 5	3 × 6
7 × 6	12 × 4	3 × 6	7 × 5	4 × 4	1 × 5	10 × 6	2 × 6	8 × 5	2 × 4
2 × 4	12 × 6	7 × 4	8 × 6	7 × 6	11 × 4	9 × 6	8 × 6	12 × 4	11 × 5
8 × 6	7 × 4	0 × 6	5 × 5	8 × 5	9 × 4	0 × 5	1 × 4	7 × 6	12 × 6
7 × 5	12 × 5	9 × 5	11 × 4	7 × 4	7 × 5	12 × 4	9 × 6	6 × 5	8 × 6
11 × 5	4 × 9	11 × 6	7 × 6	10 × 6	6 × 6	4 × 6	0 × 6	12 × 5	7 × 5
7 × 4	10 × 4	12 × 6	11 × 5	1 × 5	8 × 6	10 × 5	7 × 5	2 × 5	3 × 4

Started:	Finished:	Total Time:	Completed: _____ /80	Correct: _____ /80

×4, ×5, ×6 Multiplication

Name _____   Date _____

1 × 5	7 × 6	11 × 5	0 × 6	7 × 5	12 × 5	5 × 1	10 × 5	5 × 2	1 × 6
4 × 11	6 × 5	10 × 5	9 × 5	6 × 11	5 × 11	4 × 1	11 × 4	5 × 3	4 × 0
9 × 4	4 × 7	5 × 6	11 × 6	6 × 7	4 × 4	5 × 5	12 × 6	3 × 6	11 × 5
5 × 7	5 × 2	4 × 12	5 × 10	3 × 5	10 × 5	4 × 7	4 × 3	2 × 4	4 × 9
6 × 6	5 × 3	6 × 9	12 × 6	10 × 4	5 × 6	6 × 10	6 × 7	11 × 5	4 × 4
6 × 8	3 × 6	7 × 4	8 × 5	6 × 7	4 × 9	4 × 4	7 × 5	6 × 8	4 × 12
12 × 4	2 × 4	8 × 5	2 × 5	2 × 4	6 × 9	6 × 7	6 × 1	5 × 7	6 × 6
5 × 11	10 × 6	6 × 6	6 × 8	12 × 5	7 × 4	5 × 8	8 × 4	12 × 6	12 × 5

Started:	Finished:	Total Time:	Completed: _____ /80	Correct: _____ /80

Multiplying by 7s, 8s, and 9s

Name _____   Date _____

5 × 8	2 × 9	6 × 7	3 × 7	5 × 9	0 × 9	7 × 7	9 × 9	10 × 8	9 × 9
4 × 9	10 × 8	2 × 8	10 × 9	10 × 7	2 × 9	8 × 8	0 × 7	1 × 7	7 × 7
10 × 7	11 × 7	5 × 7	6 × 8	4 × 9	1 × 8	9 × 9	1 × 7	2 × 7	8 × 9
6 × 9	8 × 9	12 × 8	7 × 9	12 × 7	11 × 7	5 × 7	2 × 7	3 × 9	11 × 8
5 × 9	1 × 7	12 × 7	12 × 9	11 × 8	6 × 9	2 × 8	5 × 8	6 × 9	11 × 7
5 × 7	9 × 7	10 × 9	6 × 9	4 × 8	10 × 8	12 × 9	10 × 9	4 × 8	3 × 9
11 × 8	8 × 8	4 × 9	2 × 8	7 × 9	7 × 7	12 × 8	8 × 9	0 × 9	5 × 8
12 × 9	10 × 7	3 × 8	4 × 7	12 × 8	0 × 9	6 × 7	10 × 7	8 × 8	2 × 7

Started:	Finished:	Total Time:	Completed: _____ /80	Correct: _____ /80

×7, ×8, ×9 Multiplication

Name _____   Date _____

2 × 9	9 × 5	3 × 7	8 × 11	6 × 8	4 × 8	0 × 9	7 × 7	0 × 7	7 × 1
8 × 9	8 × 8	9 × 10	12 × 9	7 × 9	7 × 8	2 × 9	10 × 8	7 × 1	11 × 9
1 × 7	7 × 10	8 × 12	4 × 9	9 × 12	7 × 2	8 × 1	7 × 10	2 × 7	9 × 9
9 × 7	6 × 7	7 × 12	5 × 7	6 × 9	9 × 3	7 × 11	9 × 4	5 × 8	7 × 7
5 × 8	2 × 8	9 × 10	8 × 2	9 × 8	6 × 8	6 × 9	7 × 12	9 × 10	8 × 9
4 × 9	5 × 7	8 × 10	12 × 9	4 × 7	4 × 8	8 × 10	5 × 8	8 × 9	8 × 11
7 × 10	9 × 9	7 × 11	8 × 12	5 × 9	9 × 0	7 × 7	7 × 2	7 × 10	11 × 7
6 × 9	8 × 3	5 × 7	7 × 6	8 × 11	8 × 12	0 × 9	9 × 9	8 × 10	3 × 9

Started:	Finished:	Total Time:	Completed: _____ /80	Correct: _____ /80

Multiplying by 10s, 11s, and 12s

Name _____   Date _____

3 × 10	7 × 10	10 × 12	4 × 11	9 × 11	5 × 11	1 × 12	8 × 11	5 × 12	2 × 12
11 × 11	4 × 12	5 × 11	2 × 10	6 × 10	7 × 12	9 × 10	6 × 12	8 × 10	9 × 10
6 × 12	0 × 11	7 × 10	3 × 12	10 × 11	4 × 10	12 × 12	10 × 10	7 × 11	3 × 11
5 × 10	4 × 11	3 × 12	7 × 12	8 × 12	6 × 11	8 × 11	5 × 12	6 × 12	1 × 12
9 × 11	5 × 12	12 × 11	9 × 10	4 × 12	0 × 12	3 × 12	2 × 11	3 × 10	11 × 11
12 × 12	3 × 10	10 × 10	5 × 12	12 × 11	1 × 12	4 × 10	1 × 10	4 × 12	6 × 11
5 × 12	8 × 11	11 × 10	3 × 11	10 × 10	8 × 10	6 × 12	9 × 12	0 × 12	8 × 12
1 × 11	9 × 12	9 × 11	8 × 10	7 × 11	3 × 12	5 × 10	7 × 12	7 × 10	4 × 11

Started:	Finished:	Total Time:	Completed: _____ /80	Correct: _____ /80

×10, ×11, ×12 Multiplication

Name _____   Date _____

4 × 10	12 × 5	10 × 10	11 × 7	7 × 12	10 × 8	9 × 11	10 × 9	12 × 6	12 × 2
11 × 10	11 × 6	11 × 8	12 × 11	11 × 7	7 × 12	4 × 10	10 × 0	3 × 11	11 × 11
12 × 12	10 × 7	3 × 12	12 × 10	9 × 10	10 × 10	12 × 6	5 × 11	10 × 6	7 × 12
1 × 12	11 × 9	7 × 11	10 × 11	10 × 6	12 × 9	11 × 7	6 × 12	2 × 12	8 × 10
12 × 8	5 × 10	10 × 8	7 × 12	10 × 12	7 × 10	4 × 12	1 × 11	11 × 6	11 × 0
3 × 12	12 × 0	5 × 11	10 × 8	11 × 12	3 × 12	12 × 8	12 × 4	12 × 7	12 × 12
11 × 12	11 × 7	12 × 7	9 × 12	2 × 10	11 × 9	10 × 8	10 × 5	5 × 12	10 × 10
9 × 10	6 × 10	11 × 9	12 × 12	12 × 6	10 × 9	7 × 10	11 × 6	12 × 1	11 × 12

Started:	Finished:	Total Time:	Completed: _____ /80	Correct: _____ /80

Multiplying Across (1–3)

Name _____   Date _____

2 × 2 = _____	9 × 2 = _____	8 × 3 = _____	7 × 2 = _____	12 × 2 = _____
1 × 1 = _____	5 × 1 = _____	11 × 2 = _____	3 × 3 = _____	10 × 3 = _____
3 × 2 = _____	8 × 3 = _____	12 × 1 = _____	9 × 2 = _____	4 × 3 = _____
5 × 3 = _____	9 × 1 = _____	1 × 3 = _____	1 × 1 = _____	11 × 3 = _____
9 × 1 = _____	2 × 2 = _____	7 × 2 = _____	5 × 2 = _____	11 × 1 = _____
7 × 1 = _____	6 × 1 = _____	4 × 1 = _____	6 × 3 = _____	12 × 3 = _____
6 × 3 = _____	4 × 3 = _____	2 × 12 = _____	8 × 2 = _____	6 × 2 = _____
9 × 2 = _____	7 × 3 = _____	9 × 1 = _____	9 × 3 = _____	10 × 2 = _____
8 × 2 = _____	9 × 1 = _____	6 × 3 = _____	6 × 1 = _____	11 × 3 = _____
4 × 3 = _____	7 × 1 = _____	12 × 2 = _____	8 × 1 = _____	8 × 3 = _____
7 × 3 = _____	6 × 3 = _____	2 × 3 = _____	0 × 3 = _____	10 × 2 = _____
5 × 2 = _____	9 × 3 = _____	7 × 1 = _____	7 × 2 = _____	12 × 3 = _____
2 × 1 = _____	8 × 2 = _____	10 × 1 = _____	4 × 1 = _____	5 × 2 = _____
9 × 2 = _____	4 × 3 = _____	4 × 2 = _____	7 × 3 = _____	10 × 3 = _____
8 × 1 = _____	7 × 3 = _____	6 × 3 = _____	8 × 3 = _____	12 × 2 = _____
7 × 2 = _____	10 × 2 = _____	11 × 3 = _____	6 × 2 = _____	9 × 3 = _____

Started:	Finished:	Total Time:	Completed: _____ /80	Correct: _____ /80

Multiplying Across (1–6)

Name _____ Date _____

7 × 2 = _____	6 × 6 = _____	2 × 6 = _____	7 × 5 = _____	11 × 3 = _____
3 × 3 = _____	7 × 4 = _____	0 × 3 = _____	12 × 4 = _____	4 × 3 = _____
1 × 4 = _____	6 × 3 = _____	8 × 4 = _____	9 × 2 = _____	11 × 5 = _____
8 × 3 = _____	4 × 2 = _____	12 × 2 = _____	1 × 1 = _____	12 × 3 = _____
5 × 6 = _____	1 × 2 = _____	9 × 5 = _____	5 × 5 = _____	6 × 4 = _____
9 × 1 = _____	2 × 6 = _____	4 × 6 = _____	0 × 6 = _____	10 × 3 = _____
4 × 4 = _____	7 × 4 = _____	7 × 5 = _____	8 × 5 = _____	12 × 1 = _____
2 × 5 = _____	6 × 5 = _____	7 × 6 = _____	9 × 3 = _____	5 × 4 = _____
7 × 3 = _____	5 × 2 = _____	5 × 5 = _____	6 × 1 = _____	11 × 4 = _____
10 × 2 = _____	12 × 5 = _____	1 × 5 = _____	3 × 4 = _____	5 × 5 = _____
3 × 6 = _____	8 × 6 = _____	8 × 3 = _____	8 × 2 = _____	10 × 6 = _____
0 × 6 = _____	9 × 6 = _____	6 × 6 = _____	6 × 5 = _____	12 × 6 = _____
8 × 6 = _____	1 × 5 = _____	3 × 1 = _____	10 × 4 = _____	8 × 5 = _____
5 × 5 = _____	7 × 3 = _____	0 × 6 = _____	3 × 5 = _____	10 × 5 = _____
2 × 4 = _____	4 × 5 = _____	7 × 3 = _____	2 × 6 = _____	12 × 4 = _____
0 × 5 = _____	7 × 6 = _____	11 × 6 = _____	9 × 5 = _____	9 × 6 = _____

Started:	Finished:	Total Time:	Completed: _____ /80	Correct: _____ /80

Multiplying Across (1–9)

Name _____ Date _____

$10 \times 7 =$ ___	$9 \times 2 =$ ___	$6 \times 6 =$ ___	$7 \times 4 =$ ___	$10 \times 3 =$ ___
$11 \times 5 =$ ___	$7 \times 6 =$ ___	$4 \times 2 =$ ___	$12 \times 1 =$ ___	$8 \times 8 =$ ___
$12 \times 2 =$ ___	$8 \times 3 =$ ___	$3 \times 9 =$ ___	$4 \times 3 =$ ___	$11 \times 4 =$ ___
$11 \times 9 =$ ___	$6 \times 2 =$ ___	$7 \times 4 =$ ___	$9 \times 6 =$ ___	$12 \times 3 =$ ___
$12 \times 5 =$ ___	$11 \times 2 =$ ___	$9 \times 5 =$ ___	$8 \times 4 =$ ___	$7 \times 3 =$ ___
$12 \times 6 =$ ___	$4 \times 9 =$ ___	$11 \times 8 =$ ___	$3 \times 8 =$ ___	$11 \times 5 =$ ___
$10 \times 5 =$ ___	$5 \times 1 =$ ___	$6 \times 7 =$ ___	$8 \times 1 =$ ___	$12 \times 2 =$ ___
$12 \times 4 =$ ___	$8 \times 7 =$ ___	$9 \times 4 =$ ___	$3 \times 6 =$ ___	$11 \times 7 =$ ___
$10 \times 3 =$ ___	$2 \times 3 =$ ___	$0 \times 5 =$ ___	$12 \times 7 =$ ___	$6 \times 7 =$ ___
$11 \times 1 =$ ___	$6 \times 4 =$ ___	$2 \times 9 =$ ___	$5 \times 2 =$ ___	$10 \times 6 =$ ___
$12 \times 7 =$ ___	$11 \times 9 =$ ___	$5 \times 6 =$ ___	$9 \times 7 =$ ___	$7 \times 9 =$ ___
$10 \times 6 =$ ___	$8 \times 5 =$ ___	$3 \times 5 =$ ___	$6 \times 4 =$ ___	$2 \times 6 =$ ___
$12 \times 1 =$ ___	$1 \times 7 =$ ___	$6 \times 9 =$ ___	$2 \times 9 =$ ___	$10 \times 5 =$ ___
$11 \times 4 =$ ___	$4 \times 4 =$ ___	$12 \times 4 =$ ___	$5 \times 3 =$ ___	$7 \times 8 =$ ___
$11 \times 7 =$ ___	$5 \times 5 =$ ___	$1 \times 9 =$ ___	$5 \times 7 =$ ___	$10 \times 7 =$ ___
$12 \times 3 =$ ___	$3 \times 3 =$ ___	$8 \times 6 =$ ___	$6 \times 6 =$ ___	$11 \times 6 =$ ___

Started:	Finished:	Total Time:	Completed: _____ /80	Correct: _____ /80

Multiplying Across (1–12)

Name _____ Date _____

3 × 3 = _____	10 × 10 = ____	6 × 6 = _____	12 × 12 = ____	5 × 5 = _____
4 × 4 = _____	11 × 11 = ____	7 × 7 = _____	9 × 9 = _____	12 × 10 = ____
7 × 7 = _____	10 × 9 = ____	1 × 1 = _____	11 × 10 = ____	2 × 2 = _____
5 × 5 = _____	4 × 11 = ____	3 × 3 = _____	10 × 9 = ____	8 × 8 = _____
8 × 6 = _____	12 × 7 = ____	8 × 12 = ____	6 × 6 = _____	9 × 7 = _____
9 × 4 = _____	5 × 10 = ____	4 × 2 = _____	4 × 12 = ____	3 × 5 = _____
11 × 7 = _____	7 × 6 = _____	2 × 9 = _____	12 × 5 = ____	5 × 6 = _____
2 × 7 = _____	4 × 12 = ____	1 × 8 = _____	4 × 11 = ____	8 × 2 = _____
5 × 8 = _____	11 × 6 = ____	9 × 0 = _____	11 × 5 = ____	6 × 8 = _____
4 × 6 = _____	12 × 2 = ____	3 × 6 = _____	4 × 10 = ____	1 × 8 = _____
9 × 3 = _____	6 × 10 = ____	5 × 9 = _____	9 × 11 = ____	7 × 6 = _____
9 × 6 = _____	8 × 11 = ____	7 × 2 = _____	3 × 4 = _____	12 × 6 = ____
0 × 2 = _____	12 × 9 = ____	5 × 4 = _____	12 × 3 = ____	5 × 5 = _____
3 × 12 = ____	5 × 4 = _____	8 × 9 = _____	0 × 11 = ____	8 × 7 = _____
7 × 4 = _____	8 × 10 = ____	4 × 5 = _____	10 × 5 = ____	6 × 3 = _____
6 × 9 = _____	10 × 7 = ____	6 × 5 = _____	12 × 7 = ____	9 × 5 = _____

Started:	Finished:	Total Time:	Completed: _____ /80	Correct: _____ /80

Answers Up to 50

Name _____   Date _____

10 × 5	6 × 8	4 × 9	2 × 11	12 × 4	5 × 5	2 × 10	4 × 6	9 × 2	8 × 6
5 × 8	7 × 7	12 × 1	10 × 3	6 × 6	6 × 2	9 × 5	3 × 7	4 × 1	3 × 9
7 × 6	11 × 2	5 × 4	8 × 5	1 × 1	8 × 1	4 × 3	5 × 8	5 × 6	11 × 0
2 × 9	4 × 10	8 × 6	6 × 7	4 × 4	11 × 3	6 × 2	7 × 6	4 × 8	4 × 12
12 × 3	4 × 5	5 × 10	4 × 12	5 × 5	2 × 9	4 × 5	7 × 4	4 × 10	6 × 1
4 × 11	3 × 6	7 × 5	6 × 5	3 × 3	7 × 5	6 × 3	2 × 5	11 × 2	7 × 3
6 × 6	7 × 4	3 × 4	12 × 1	2 × 2	9 × 3	1 × 7	10 × 4	2 × 12	1 × 12
8 × 3	5 × 9	9 × 3	3 × 11	7 × 7	4 × 8	8 × 0	3 × 9	3 × 12	4 × 10

Started:	Finished:	Total Time:	Completed: _____ /80	Correct: _____ /80

Answers Across Up to 50

Name _____ Date _____

2 × 12 = _____	7 × 1 = _____	4 × 5 = _____	4 × 4 = _____	11 × 1 = _____
6 × 3 = _____	12 × 3 = _____	5 × 5 = _____	8 × 5 = _____	10 × 0 = _____
11 × 2 = _____	8 × 5 = _____	6 × 0 = _____	3 × 4 = _____	3 × 12 = _____
4 × 10 = _____	9 × 1 = _____	4 × 4 = _____	9 × 5 = _____	2 × 11 = _____
11 × 0 = _____	5 × 6 = _____	5 × 2 = _____	10 × 4 = _____	4 × 2 = _____
1 × 12 = _____	9 × 4 = _____	6 × 7 = _____	7 × 7 = _____	5 × 10 = _____
10 × 5 = _____	5 × 7 = _____	11 × 3 = _____	2 × 2 = _____	3 × 8 = _____
3 × 11 = _____	4 × 9 = _____	2 × 6 = _____	6 × 6 = _____	10 × 1 = _____
2 × 12 = _____	7 × 5 = _____	5 × 9 = _____	0 × 9 = _____	4 × 11 = _____
11 × 4 = _____	9 × 3 = _____	8 × 3 = _____	4 × 6 = _____	0 × 12 = _____
7 × 0 = _____	3 × 3 = _____	6 × 4 = _____	5 × 2 = _____	2 × 10 = _____
5 × 4 = _____	8 × 2 = _____	8 × 5 = _____	2 × 8 = _____	4 × 12 = _____
4 × 6 = _____	12 × 4 = _____	4 × 9 = _____	7 × 3 = _____	10 × 3 = _____
3 × 10 = _____	3 × 7 = _____	6 × 6 = _____	12 × 2 = _____	0 × 2 = _____
11 × 1 = _____	5 × 5 = _____	8 × 1 = _____	3 × 9 = _____	0 × 11 = _____
1 × 10 = _____	2 × 6 = _____	3 × 7 = _____	5 × 6 = _____	12 × 1 = _____

Started:	Finished:	Total Time:	Completed: _____ /80	Correct: _____ /80

Answers Up to 100

Name _____ Date _____

11 × 5	12 × 5	8 × 3	10 × 4	9 × 3	6 × 9	12 × 3	7 × 9	10 × 4	12 × 1
4 × 12	7 × 10	4 × 11	8 × 8	4 × 8	5 × 11	10 × 2	6 × 6	3 × 11	7 × 11
9 × 5	11 × 9	9 × 9	7 × 4	12 × 7	12 × 5	5 × 5	4 × 4	8 × 6	5 × 9
6 × 6	8 × 12	11 × 7	2 × 12	5 × 10	7 × 6	11 × 1	10 × 3	2 × 12	8 × 8
8 × 10	10 × 10	8 × 5	9 × 10	11 × 8	10 × 0	6 × 12	4 × 5	8 × 11	3 × 9
6 × 9	7 × 7	2 × 9	8 × 7	12 × 2	12 × 3	9 × 4	5 × 8	11 × 7	5 × 10
7 × 8	10 × 6	7 × 8	10 × 10	4 × 8	5 × 5	10 × 8	10 × 7	2 × 10	4 × 4
8 × 9	5 × 8	6 × 11	5 × 9	9 × 9	4 × 2	9 × 5	7 × 5	10 × 1	7 × 7

Started:	Finished:	Total Time:	Completed: _____ /80	Correct: _____ /80

Answers Across Up to 100

Name _____   Date _____

5 × 9 = _____	5 × 12 = _____	9 × 11 = _____	8 × 7 = _____	5 × 5 = _____
4 × 11 = _____	3 × 3 = _____	10 × 5 = _____	2 × 2 = _____	3 × 9 = _____
6 × 7 = _____	12 × 1 = _____	9 × 9 = _____	12 × 7 = _____	7 × 1 = _____
7 × 8 = _____	3 × 11 = _____	6 × 10 = _____	4 × 4 = _____	5 × 6 = _____
9 × 5 = _____	10 × 10 = _____	9 × 4 = _____	6 × 6 = _____	6 × 12 = _____
6 × 8 = _____	11 × 7 = _____	11 × 2 = _____	8 × 8 = _____	6 × 8 = _____
9 × 4 = _____	12 × 6 = _____	11 × 8 = _____	5 × 5 = _____	5 × 3 = _____
7 × 5 = _____	10 × 5 = _____	3 × 12 = _____	6 × 2 = _____	7 × 2 = _____
12 × 7 = _____	6 × 8 = _____	11 × 6 = _____	3 × 8 = _____	9 × 8 = _____
8 × 5 = _____	9 × 10 = _____	7 × 10 = _____	7 × 7 = _____	5 × 5 = _____
4 × 7 = _____	8 × 12 = _____	5 × 11 = _____	5 × 4 = _____	4 × 4 = _____
8 × 8 = _____	11 × 6 = _____	0 × 0 = _____	9 × 8 = _____	4 × 12 = _____
8 × 9 = _____	10 × 7 = _____	1 × 10 = _____	7 × 6 = _____	6 × 1 = _____
12 × 3 = _____	6 × 3 = _____	10 × 10 = _____	8 × 5 = _____	1 × 9 = _____
2 × 7 = _____	10 × 6 = _____	10 × 8 = _____	3 × 3 = _____	5 × 7 = _____
9 × 6 = _____	11 × 8 = _____	11 × 2 = _____	6 × 4 = _____	9 × 6 = _____

Started:	Finished:	Total Time:	Completed: _____ /80	Correct: _____ /80

Test #1

Name _____ Date _____

10 × 2	4 × 8	3 × 3	3 × 8	11 × 5	9 × 9	11 × 3	12 × 5	4 × 7	10 × 12
3 × 8	2 × 6	2 × 10	10 × 10	3 × 9	6 × 12	8 × 10	5 × 6	8 × 4	11 × 12
9 × 5	10 × 7	4 × 9	9 × 11	10 × 4	2 × 7	6 × 9	10 × 8	5 × 10	9 × 7
12 × 1	5 × 9	9 × 7	8 × 7	6 × 5	4 × 4	5 × 12	3 × 10	10 × 11	8 × 8
11 × 7	6 × 11	5 × 5	6 × 12	2 × 2	5 × 5	11 × 7	8 × 4	11 × 1	12 × 5
5 × 8	7 × 7	8 × 8	4 × 4	4 × 7	5 × 9	12 × 4	6 × 3	8 × 12	4 × 11
6 × 6	11 × 11	6 × 9	2 × 9	9 × 3	6 × 6	3 × 8	9 × 7	12 × 11	12 × 3
8 × 9	3 × 12	12 × 12	8 × 6	12 × 8	10 × 5	9 × 12	5 × 4	6 × 5	11 × 10

Started: _____ Finished: _____ Total Time: _____ Completed: _____ /80 Correct: _____ /80

Test #2

Name _____   Date _____

3 × 3	5 × 12	6 × 6	12 × 12	8 × 3	6 × 5	11 × 1	12 × 10	6 × 8	9 × 9
6 × 5	11 × 7	10 × 5	3 × 8	9 × 2	12 × 6	9 × 10	11 × 5	7 × 3	12 × 12
10 × 12	10 × 5	2 × 8	10 × 10	6 × 11	8 × 11	3 × 12	8 × 4	11 × 11	2 × 5
11 × 12	11 × 3	4 × 4	4 × 10	12 × 7	7 × 9	4 × 11	10 × 9	3 × 12	12 × 1
9 × 7	8 × 10	5 × 5	10 × 7	11 × 11	3 × 7	10 × 5	7 × 7	12 × 5	11 × 5
8 × 8	6 × 9	5 × 9	9 × 11	6 × 4	11 × 10	11 × 9	5 × 4	3 × 10	4 × 1
12 × 5	12 × 4	11 × 3	8 × 7	10 × 9	9 × 11	6 × 7	6 × 8	12 × 4	12 × 5
4 × 11	10 × 10	4 × 6	6 × 12	12 × 10	12 × 7	12 × 8	5 × 5	8 × 7	4 × 11

Started:	Finished:	Total Time:	Completed: _____ /80	Correct: _____ /80

Test #3

Name _____   Date _____

5 × 6	6 × 3	7 × 7	11 × 9	12 × 6	6 × 2	8 × 3	10 × 1	4 × 3	11 × 11
8 × 12	10 × 4	12 × 5	10 × 12	10 × 2	8 × 9	9 × 3	6 × 7	7 × 4	0 × 0
11 × 3	2 × 12	3 × 9	11 × 6	7 × 10	9 × 1	3 × 12	9 × 6	6 × 6	3 × 3
7 × 9	9 × 10	10 × 7	2 × 9	3 × 8	5 × 10	5 × 7	0 × 8	12 × 6	7 × 10
10 × 5	11 × 5	5 × 9	5 × 3	9 × 9	12 × 0	6 × 4	9 × 10	11 × 5	8 × 4
3 × 12	10 × 10	5 × 5	4 × 4	7 × 5	1 × 11	12 × 4	11 × 7	8 × 10	4 × 5
11 × 4	8 × 5	6 × 4	12 × 11	10 × 10	7 × 9	8 × 12	12 × 12	5 × 7	6 × 5
8 × 9	12 × 7	10 × 11	5 × 10	6 × 9	4 × 5	10 × 9	8 × 8	10 × 6	4 × 8

Started:	Finished:	Total Time:	Completed: _____ /80	Correct: _____ /80

Test #4

Name _____ Date _____

5 × 8	11 × 10	8 × 9	6 × 12	2 × 10	12 × 12	6 × 9	11 × 7	8 × 4	11 × 1
4 × 4	2 × 9	4 × 8	9 × 7	10 × 2	3 × 8	9 × 11	12 × 4	6 × 3	8 × 12
11 × 11	8 × 6	9 × 5	5 × 5	11 × 8	10 × 10	8 × 7	3 × 8	9 × 7	12 × 11
3 × 12	11 × 5	12 × 1	2 × 6	4 × 7	5 × 9	6 × 12	9 × 12	5 × 4	6 × 5
3 × 3	3 × 9	11 × 7	10 × 7	9 × 3	6 × 6	2 × 7	12 × 5	4 × 7	10 × 12
12 × 5	10 × 4	4 × 9	5 × 9	12 × 8	10 × 5	4 × 4	5 × 6	8 × 4	11 × 12
4 × 11	6 × 5	2 × 2	6 × 11	8 × 8	11 × 3	5 × 5	10 × 8	5 × 10	9 × 7
12 × 3	6 × 6	9 × 9	7 × 7	6 × 9	8 × 10	5 × 12	3 × 10	10 × 11	8 × 8

Started:	Finished:	Total Time:	Completed: _____ /80	Correct: _____ /80

Test #5

Name _____   Date _____

5	12	9	10	4	2	5	11	12	9
× 5	× 12	× 6	× 8	× 7	× 2	× 10	× 11	× 1	× 12

6	3	0	3	5	12	12	10	6	10
× 4	× 8	× 8	× 12	× 10	× 6	× 4	× 12	× 10	× 10

10	10	9	11	12	5	6	6	12	5
× 11	× 10	× 10	× 12	× 6	× 5	× 7	× 9	× 8	× 9

11	5	11	9	8	9	7	8	10	9
× 9	× 9	× 7	× 10	× 7	× 9	× 10	× 7	× 3	× 7

10	6	2	12	2	12	11	5	4	7
× 12	× 6	× 12	× 5	× 7	× 3	× 3	× 12	× 7	× 2

11	10	8	11	6	0	9	10	6	10
× 6	× 5	× 8	× 6	× 8	× 11	× 8	× 6	× 6	× 8

2	11	4	10	7	10	2	4	8	4
× 9	× 3	× 3	× 7	× 5	× 5	× 10	× 8	× 8	× 12

5	8	7	11	5	12	5	5	7	12
× 3	× 10	× 4	× 9	× 11	× 7	× 9	× 11	× 7	× 9

Started:	Finished:	Total Time:	Completed: _____ /80	Correct: _____ /80

Test #6

Name _____ Date _____

4 × 4 = _____	0 × 9 = _____	3 × 9 = _____	10 × 2 = _____	11 × 7 = _____
5 × 5 = _____	4 × 8 = _____	11 × 11 = _____	7 × 4 = _____	5 × 12 = _____
12 × 12 = _____	9 × 6 = _____	8 × 7 = _____	11 × 5 = _____	4 × 7 = _____
7 × 5 = _____	4 × 9 = _____	9 × 2 = _____	9 × 12 = _____	9 × 11 = _____
10 × 8 = _____	3 × 5 = _____	8 × 8 = _____	10 × 7 = _____	8 × 6 = _____
2 × 5 = _____	7 × 6 = _____	5 × 7 = _____	12 × 11 = _____	12 × 6 = _____
9 × 8 = _____	2 × 7 = _____	7 × 6 = _____	4 × 12 = _____	11 × 10 = _____
6 × 4 = _____	2 × 5 = _____	9 × 9 = _____	3 × 11 = _____	10 × 12 = _____
3 × 7 = _____	6 × 10 = _____	1 × 8 = _____	10 × 6 = _____	3 × 9 = _____
9 × 9 = _____	0 × 4 = _____	6 × 5 = _____	7 × 11 = _____	5 × 11 = _____
6 × 5 = _____	1 × 9 = _____	3 × 7 = _____	12 × 12 = _____	10 × 3 = _____
8 × 4 = _____	6 × 7 = _____	10 × 9 = _____	4 × 4 = _____	12 × 7 = _____
3 × 6 = _____	9 × 7 = _____	2 × 8 = _____	7 × 10 = _____	10 × 10 = _____
8 × 9 = _____	12 × 5 = _____	9 × 5 = _____	8 × 8 = _____	3 × 12 = _____
7 × 7 = _____	6 × 5 = _____	3 × 9 = _____	12 × 6 = _____	11 × 11 = _____
9 × 6 = _____	3 × 8 = _____	6 × 6 = _____	4 × 11 = _____	12 × 8 = _____

Started:	Finished:	Total Time:	Completed: _____ /80	Correct: _____ /80

Test #7

5 × 12 = _____	3 × 12 = _____	2 × 6 = _____	7 × 7 = _____	0 × 0 = _____
3 × 11 = _____	8 × 8 = _____	0 × 9 = _____	11 × 11 = _____	6 × 9 = _____
12 × 12 = _____	6 × 10 = _____	4 × 8 = _____	3 × 9 = _____	7 × 1 = _____
2 × 9 = _____	5 × 11 = _____	9 × 6 = _____	4 × 8 = _____	10 × 9 = _____
11 × 4 = _____	0 × 12 = _____	7 × 5 = _____	9 × 7 = _____	1 × 8 = _____
10 × 6 = _____	10 × 3 = _____	8 × 6 = _____	7 × 6 = _____	4 × 3 = _____
7 × 11 = _____	12 × 7 = _____	2 × 5 = _____	5 × 7 = _____	6 × 6 = _____
10 × 10 = _____	4 × 12 = _____	9 × 8 = _____	4 × 3 = _____	9 × 0 = _____
9 × 11 = _____	3 × 11 = _____	6 × 4 = _____	1 × 6 = _____	7 × 9 = _____
10 × 8 = _____	3 × 7 = _____	10 × 6 = _____	7 × 8 = _____	9 × 1 = _____
7 × 4 = _____	12 × 8 = _____	9 × 9 = _____	9 × 0 = _____	12 × 6 = _____
11 × 10 = _____	11 × 11 = _____	6 × 5 = _____	8 × 2 = _____	1 × 8 = _____
10 × 7 = _____	5 × 7 = _____	8 × 4 = _____	9 × 9 = _____	11 × 5 = _____
6 × 2 = _____	9 × 12 = _____	3 × 6 = _____	11 × 12 = _____	6 × 7 = _____
12 × 6 = _____	10 × 7 = _____	8 × 9 = _____	4 × 1 = _____	6 × 8 = _____
10 × 10 = _____	12 × 11 = _____	7 × 7 = _____	3 × 7 = _____	9 × 2 = _____

Started:	Finished:	Total Time:	Completed: _____ /80	Correct: _____ /80

Test #8

Name _____ Date _____

$10 \times 4 =$ _____ $0 \times 9 =$ _____ $2 \times 9 =$ _____ $6 \times 8 =$ _____ $12 \times 3 =$ _____

$7 \times 12 =$ _____ $3 \times 8 =$ _____ $4 \times 4 =$ _____ $7 \times 7 =$ _____ $4 \times 10 =$ _____

$9 \times 11 =$ _____ $4 \times 5 =$ _____ $8 \times 5 =$ _____ $4 \times 9 =$ _____ $10 \times 10 =$ _____

$10 \times 3 =$ _____ $6 \times 2 =$ _____ $3 \times 3 =$ _____ $11 \times 11 =$ _____ $0 \times 2 =$ _____

$8 \times 12 =$ _____ $3 \times 1 =$ _____ $12 \times 12 =$ _____ $9 \times 1 =$ _____ $4 \times 8 =$ _____

$11 \times 6 =$ _____ $2 \times 8 =$ _____ $2 \times 6 =$ _____ $3 \times 6 =$ _____ $12 \times 4 =$ _____

$10 \times 7 =$ _____ $0 \times 6 =$ _____ $7 \times 3 =$ _____ $5 \times 5 =$ _____ $10 \times 9 =$ _____

$2 \times 10 =$ _____ $1 \times 8 =$ _____ $11 \times 7 =$ _____ $4 \times 2 =$ _____ $2 \times 3 =$ _____

$5 \times 12 =$ _____ $4 \times 4 =$ _____ $6 \times 9 =$ _____ $3 \times 7 =$ _____ $12 \times 3 =$ _____

$11 \times 2 =$ _____ $7 \times 5 =$ _____ $8 \times 1 =$ _____ $5 \times 2 =$ _____ $4 \times 11 =$ _____

$2 \times 9 =$ _____ $12 \times 10 =$ _____ $5 \times 9 =$ _____ $8 \times 8 =$ _____ $10 \times 5 =$ _____

$10 \times 11 =$ _____ $3 \times 3 =$ _____ $7 \times 7 =$ _____ $6 \times 4 =$ _____ $12 \times 8 =$ _____

$12 \times 9 =$ _____ $4 \times 4 =$ _____ $3 \times 7 =$ _____ $9 \times 6 =$ _____ $4 \times 11 =$ _____

$9 \times 1 =$ _____ $12 \times 12 =$ _____ $5 \times 5 =$ _____ $12 \times 7 =$ _____ $7 \times 4 =$ _____

$10 \times 10 =$ _____ $6 \times 6 =$ _____ $6 \times 7 =$ _____ $2 \times 9 =$ _____ $5 \times 12 =$ _____

$11 \times 7 =$ _____ $8 \times 8 =$ _____ $8 \times 4 =$ _____ $7 \times 5 =$ _____ $9 \times 10 =$ _____

| Started: | Finished: | Total Time: | Completed: _____/80 | Correct: _____/80 |

Test #9

Name _____ Date _____

3 × 7 = _____	2 × 6 = _____	5 × 5 = _____	12 × 3 = _____	11 × 11 = _____
9 × 3 = _____	11 × 12 = _____	4 × 7 = _____	7 × 11 = _____	6 × 5 = _____
5 × 6 = _____	3 × 4 = _____	9 × 9 = _____	10 × 6 = _____	12 × 12 = _____
10 × 10 = _____	1 × 1 = _____	3 × 3 = _____	6 × 12 = _____	8 × 4 = _____
7 × 3 = _____	8 × 8 = _____	2 × 6 = _____	12 × 8 = _____	10 × 12 = _____
9 × 6 = _____	3 × 8 = _____	9 × 2 = _____	4 × 11 = _____	7 × 12 = _____
8 × 1 = _____	4 × 3 = _____	12 × 12 = _____	8 × 5 = _____	6 × 11 = _____
9 × 9 = _____	7 × 7 = _____	3 × 9 = _____	11 × 9 = _____	12 × 4 = _____
10 × 10 = _____	1 × 9 = _____	7 × 7 = _____	2 × 2 = _____	4 × 10 = _____
5 × 1 = _____	5 × 5 = _____	6 × 6 = _____	10 × 7 = _____	10 × 0 = _____
6 × 9 = _____	12 × 2 = _____	7 × 1 = _____	12 × 5 = _____	6 × 4 = _____
4 × 4 = _____	8 × 0 = _____	5 × 5 = _____	4 × 12 = _____	12 × 8 = _____
5 × 8 = _____	9 × 7 = _____	2 × 7 = _____	5 × 10 = _____	10 × 2 = _____
3 × 10 = _____	7 × 4 = _____	8 × 2 = _____	2 × 11 = _____	6 × 7 = _____
7 × 5 = _____	4 × 6 = _____	6 × 8 = _____	11 × 8 = _____	4 × 10 = _____
8 × 3 = _____	9 × 9 = _____	8 × 8 = _____	6 × 10 = _____	11 × 4 = _____

Started:	Finished:	Total Time:	Completed: _____ /80	Correct: _____ /80

Answer Keys (pages 5–8)

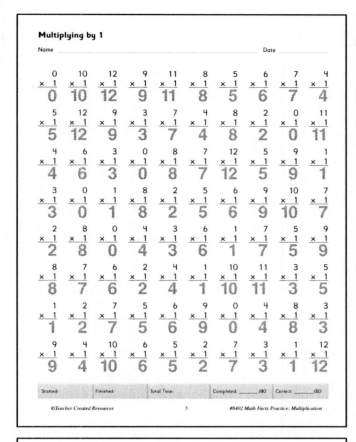

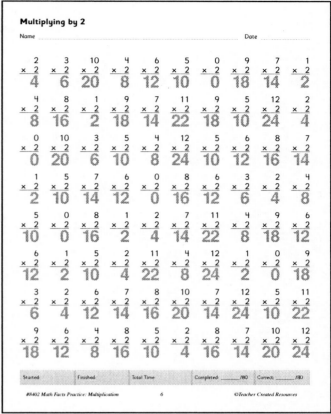

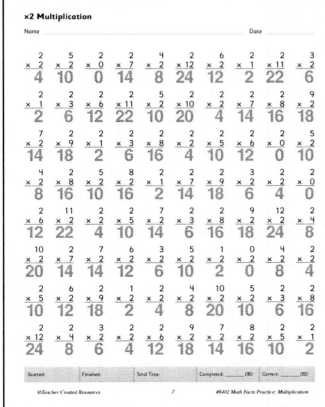

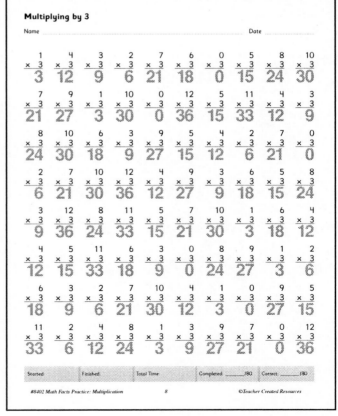

Answer Keys (pages 9–12)

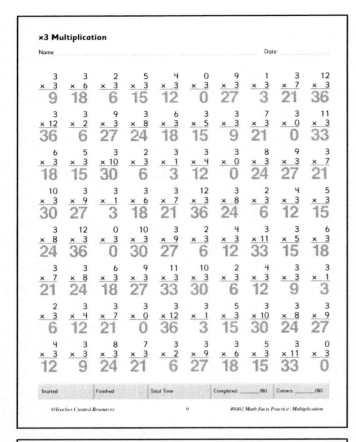

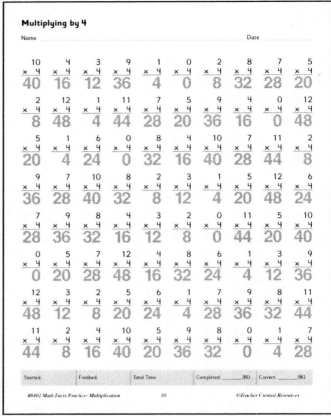

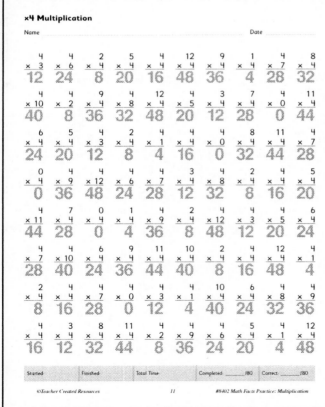

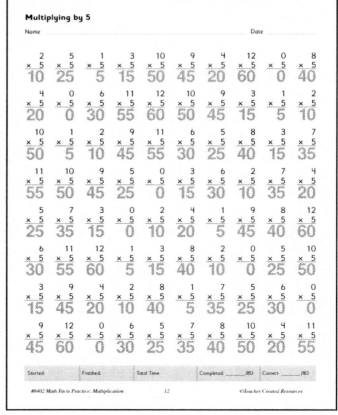

Answer Keys (pages 13–16)

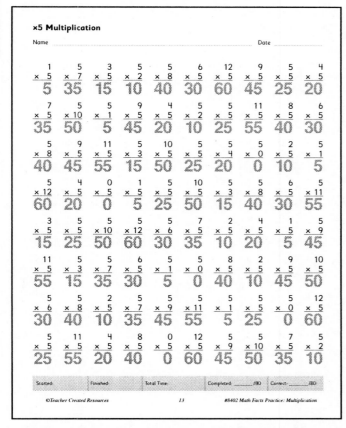

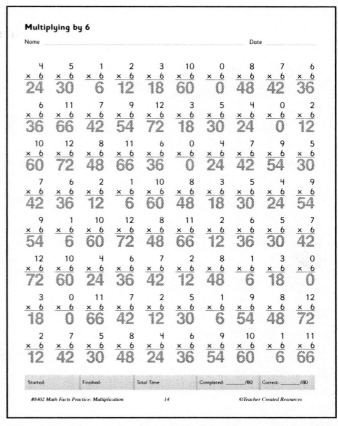

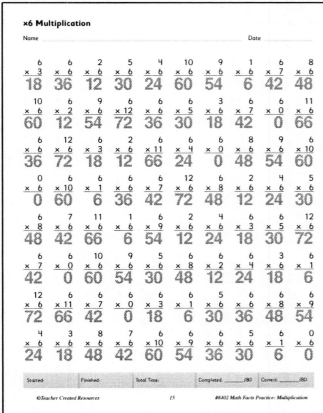

Answer Keys (pages 17–20)

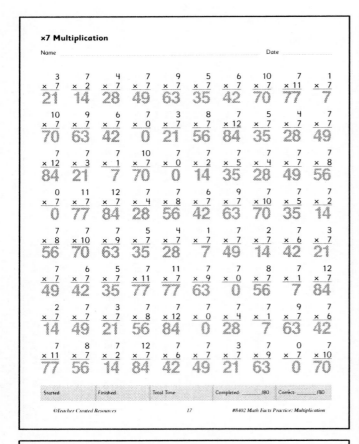

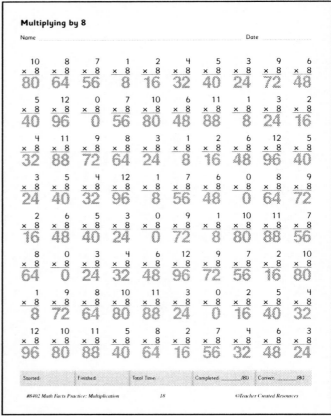

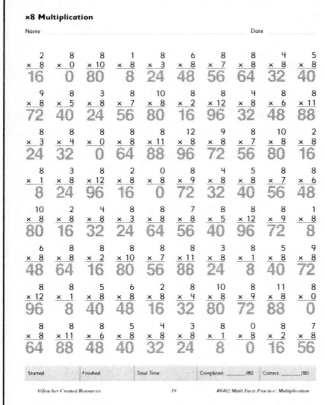

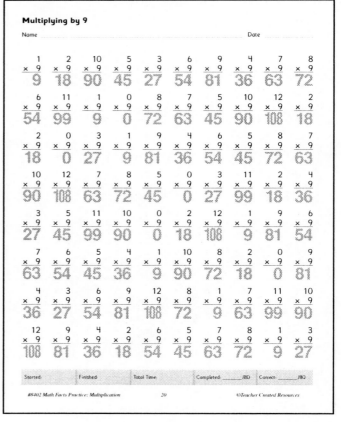

Answer Keys (pages 21–24)

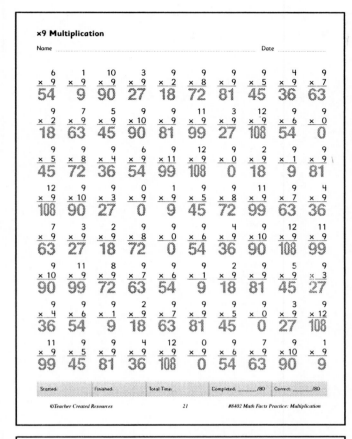

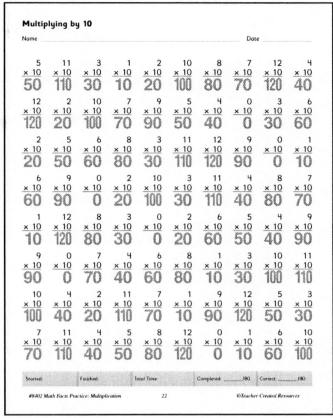

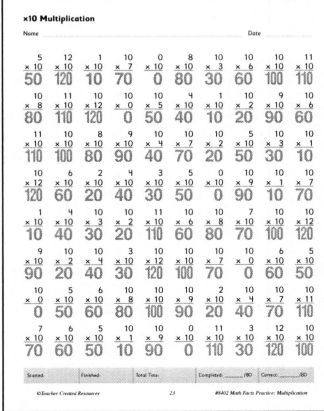

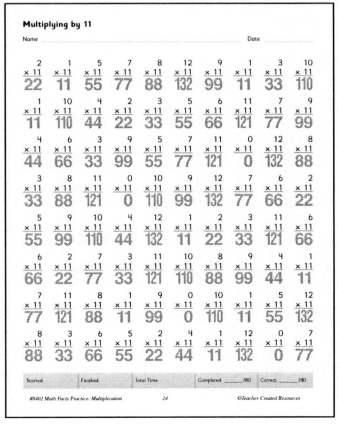

Answer Keys (pages 25–28)

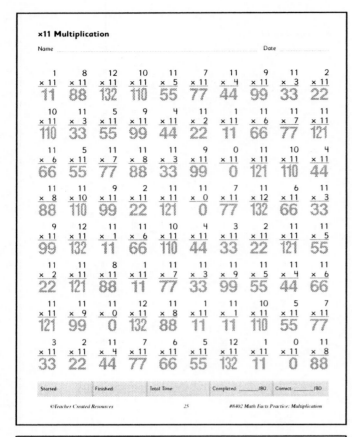

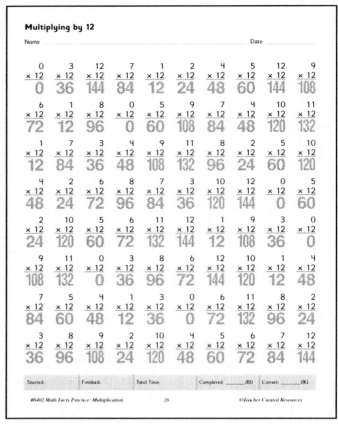

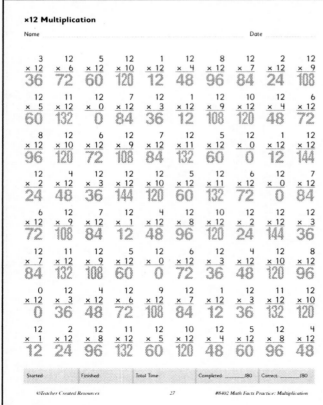

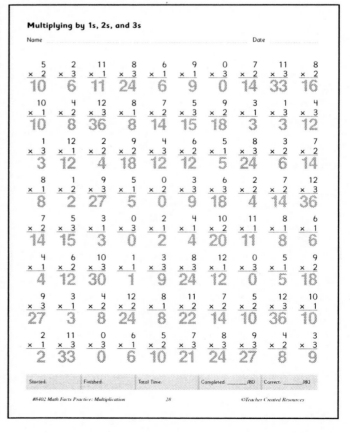

Answer Keys (pages 29–32)

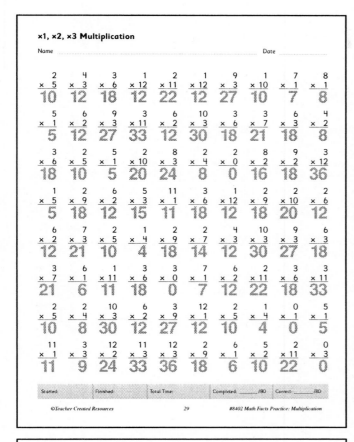

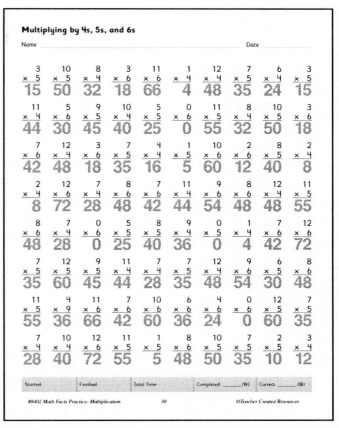

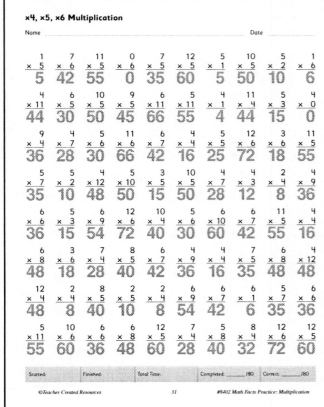

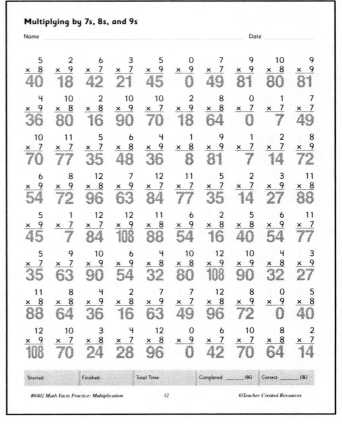

Answer Keys (pages 33–36)

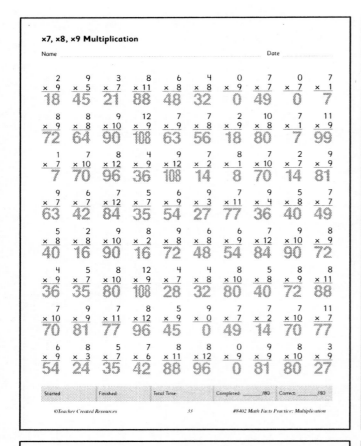

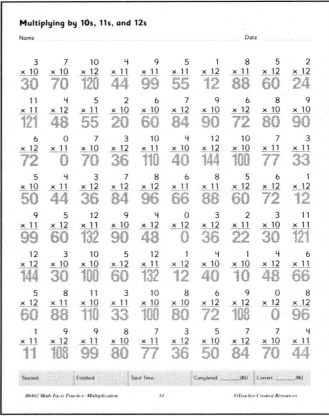

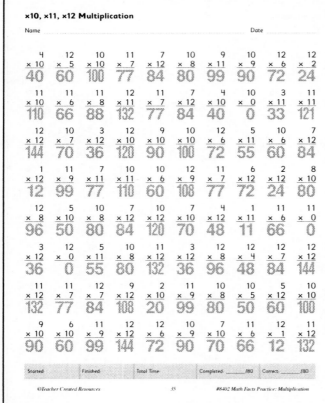

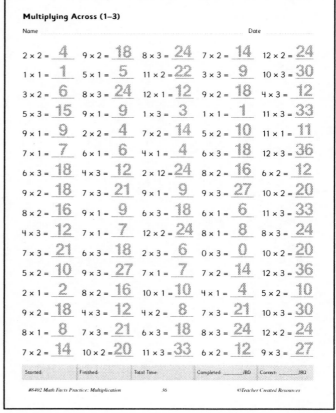

Answer Keys (pages 37–40)

Multiplying Across (1–6)

Name _____   Date _____

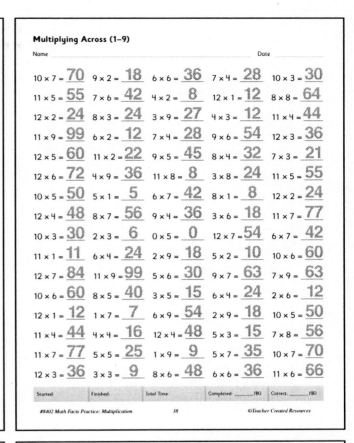

7 × 2 = 14	6 × 6 = 36	2 × 6 = 12	7 × 5 = 35	11 × 3 = 33
3 × 3 = 9	7 × 4 = 28	0 × 3 = 0	12 × 4 = 48	4 × 3 = 12
1 × 4 = 4	6 × 3 = 18	8 × 4 = 32	9 × 2 = 18	11 × 5 = 55
8 × 3 = 24	4 × 2 = 8	12 × 2 = 24	1 × 1 = 1	12 × 3 = 36
5 × 6 = 30	1 × 2 = 2	9 × 5 = 45	5 × 5 = 25	6 × 4 = 24
9 × 1 = 9	2 × 6 = 12	4 × 6 = 24	0 × 6 = 0	10 × 3 = 30
4 × 4 = 16	7 × 4 = 28	7 × 5 = 35	8 × 5 = 40	12 × 1 = 12
2 × 5 = 10	6 × 5 = 30	7 × 6 = 42	9 × 3 = 27	5 × 4 = 20
7 × 3 = 21	5 × 2 = 10	5 × 5 = 25	6 × 1 = 6	11 × 4 = 44
10 × 2 = 20	12 × 5 = 60	1 × 5 = 5	3 × 4 = 12	5 × 5 = 25
3 × 6 = 18	8 × 6 = 48	8 × 3 = 24	8 × 2 = 16	10 × 6 = 60
0 × 6 = 0	9 × 6 = 54	6 × 6 = 36	6 × 5 = 30	12 × 6 = 72
8 × 6 = 48	1 × 5 = 5	3 × 1 = 3	10 × 4 = 40	8 × 5 = 40
5 × 5 = 25	7 × 3 = 21	0 × 6 = 0	3 × 5 = 15	10 × 5 = 50
2 × 4 = 8	4 × 5 = 20	7 × 3 = 21	2 × 6 = 12	12 × 4 = 48
0 × 5 = 0	7 × 6 = 42	11 × 6 = 66	9 × 5 = 45	9 × 6 = 54

Started: _____ Finished: _____ Total Time: _____ Completed: _____ /80 Correct: _____ /80

Multiplying Across (1–9)

Name _____   Date _____

10 × 7 = 70	9 × 2 = 18	6 × 6 = 36	7 × 4 = 28	10 × 3 = 30
11 × 5 = 55	7 × 6 = 42	4 × 2 = 8	12 × 1 = 12	8 × 8 = 64
12 × 2 = 24	8 × 3 = 24	3 × 9 = 27	4 × 3 = 12	11 × 4 = 44
11 × 9 = 99	6 × 2 = 12	7 × 4 = 28	9 × 6 = 54	12 × 3 = 36
12 × 5 = 60	11 × 2 = 22	9 × 5 = 45	8 × 4 = 32	7 × 3 = 21
12 × 6 = 72	4 × 9 = 36	11 × 8 = 8	3 × 8 = 24	11 × 5 = 55
10 × 5 = 50	5 × 1 = 5	6 × 7 = 42	8 × 1 = 8	12 × 2 = 24
12 × 4 = 48	8 × 7 = 56	9 × 4 = 36	3 × 6 = 18	11 × 7 = 77
10 × 3 = 30	2 × 3 = 6	0 × 5 = 0	12 × 7 = 54	6 × 7 = 42
11 × 1 = 11	6 × 4 = 24	2 × 9 = 18	5 × 2 = 10	10 × 6 = 60
12 × 7 = 84	11 × 9 = 99	5 × 6 = 30	9 × 7 = 63	7 × 9 = 63
10 × 6 = 60	8 × 5 = 40	3 × 5 = 15	6 × 4 = 24	2 × 6 = 12
12 × 1 = 12	1 × 7 = 7	6 × 9 = 54	2 × 9 = 18	10 × 5 = 50
11 × 4 = 44	4 × 4 = 16	12 × 4 = 48	5 × 3 = 15	7 × 8 = 56
11 × 7 = 77	5 × 5 = 25	1 × 9 = 9	5 × 7 = 35	10 × 7 = 70
12 × 3 = 36	3 × 3 = 9	8 × 6 = 48	6 × 6 = 36	11 × 6 = 66

Started: _____ Finished: _____ Total Time: _____ Completed: _____ /80 Correct: _____ /80

Multiplying Across (1–12)

Name _____   Date _____

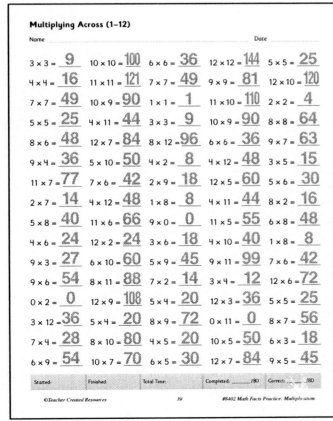

3 × 3 = 9	10 × 10 = 100	6 × 6 = 36	12 × 12 = 144	5 × 5 = 25
4 × 4 = 16	11 × 11 = 121	7 × 7 = 49	9 × 9 = 81	12 × 10 = 120
7 × 7 = 49	10 × 9 = 90	1 × 1 = 1	11 × 10 = 110	2 × 2 = 4
5 × 5 = 25	4 × 11 = 44	3 × 3 = 9	10 × 9 = 90	8 × 8 = 64
8 × 6 = 48	12 × 7 = 84	8 × 12 = 96	6 × 6 = 36	9 × 7 = 63
9 × 4 = 36	5 × 10 = 50	4 × 2 = 8	4 × 12 = 48	3 × 5 = 15
11 × 7 = 77	7 × 6 = 42	2 × 9 = 18	12 × 5 = 60	5 × 6 = 30
2 × 7 = 14	4 × 12 = 48	1 × 8 = 8	4 × 11 = 44	8 × 2 = 16
5 × 8 = 40	11 × 6 = 66	9 × 0 = 0	11 × 5 = 55	6 × 8 = 48
4 × 6 = 24	12 × 2 = 24	3 × 6 = 18	4 × 10 = 40	1 × 8 = 8
9 × 3 = 27	6 × 10 = 60	5 × 9 = 45	9 × 11 = 99	7 × 6 = 42
9 × 6 = 54	8 × 11 = 88	7 × 2 = 14	3 × 4 = 12	12 × 6 = 72
0 × 2 = 0	12 × 9 = 108	5 × 4 = 20	12 × 3 = 36	5 × 5 = 25
3 × 12 = 36	5 × 4 = 20	8 × 9 = 72	0 × 11 = 0	8 × 7 = 56
7 × 4 = 28	8 × 10 = 80	4 × 5 = 20	10 × 5 = 50	6 × 3 = 18
6 × 9 = 54	10 × 7 = 70	6 × 5 = 30	12 × 7 = 84	9 × 5 = 45

Started: _____ Finished: _____ Total Time: _____ Completed: _____ /80 Correct: _____ /80

Answers Up to 50

Name _____   Date _____

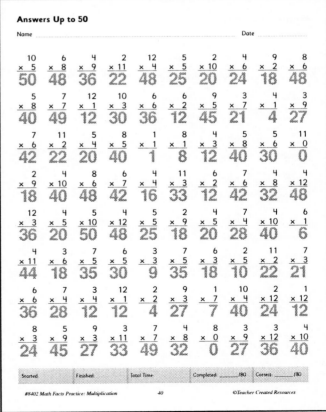

10 × 5 = 50	6 × 8 = 48	4 × 9 = 36	2 × 11 = 22	12 × 4 = 48	5 × 5 = 25	2 × 10 = 20	4 × 6 = 24	9 × 2 = 18	8 × 6 = 48
5 × 8 = 40	7 × 7 = 49	12 × 1 = 12	10 × 3 = 30	6 × 6 = 36	6 × 2 = 12	9 × 5 = 45	3 × 7 = 21	4 × 1 = 4	3 × 9 = 27
7 × 6 = 42	11 × 2 = 22	5 × 4 = 20	8 × 5 = 40	1 × 1 = 1	8 × 1 = 8	4 × 3 = 12	5 × 8 = 40	5 × 6 = 30	11 × 0 = 0
2 × 9 = 18	4 × 10 = 40	8 × 6 = 48	6 × 7 = 42	4 × 4 = 16	11 × 3 = 33	6 × 2 = 12	7 × 6 = 42	4 × 8 = 32	4 × 12 = 48
12 × 3 = 36	4 × 5 = 20	5 × 10 = 50	4 × 12 = 48	5 × 5 = 25	2 × 9 = 18	5 × 4 = 20	7 × 4 = 28	4 × 10 = 40	6 × 1 = 6
4 × 11 = 44	3 × 6 = 18	7 × 5 = 35	6 × 5 = 30	3 × 3 = 9	7 × 5 = 35	6 × 3 = 18	2 × 5 = 10	11 × 2 = 22	7 × 3 = 21
6 × 6 = 36	7 × 4 = 28	3 × 4 = 12	12 × 1 = 12	2 × 2 = 4	9 × 3 = 27	1 × 7 = 7	10 × 4 = 40	2 × 12 = 24	1 × 12 = 12
8 × 3 = 24	5 × 9 = 45	9 × 3 = 27	3 × 11 = 33	7 × 7 = 49	4 × 8 = 32	8 × 0 = 0	3 × 9 = 27	3 × 12 = 36	4 × 10 = 40

Started: _____ Finished: _____ Total Time: _____ Completed: _____ /80 Correct: _____ /80

Answer Keys (pages 41–44)

Answers Across Up to 50

Name _____ Date _____

2 × 12 = 24   7 × 1 = 7   4 × 5 = 20   4 × 4 = 16   11 × 1 = 11
6 × 3 = 18   12 × 3 = 36 5 × 5 = 25   8 × 5 = 40   10 × 0 = 0
11 × 2 = 22   8 × 5 = 40   6 × 0 = 0   3 × 4 = 12   3 × 12 = 36
4 × 10 = 40   9 × 1 = 9   4 × 4 = 16   9 × 5 = 45   2 × 11 = 22
11 × 0 = 0   5 × 6 = 30   5 × 2 = 10   10 × 4 = 40 4 × 2 = 8
1 × 12 = 12   9 × 4 = 36   6 × 7 = 42   7 × 7 = 49   5 × 10 = 50
10 × 5 = 50   5 × 7 = 35   11 × 3 = 24 2 × 2 = 4   3 × 8 = 24
3 × 11 = 33   4 × 9 = 36   2 × 6 = 12   6 × 6 = 36   10 × 1 = 10
2 × 12 = 24   7 × 5 = 35   5 × 9 = 45   0 × 9 = 0   4 × 11 = 44
11 × 4 = 44   9 × 3 = 27   8 × 3 = 24   4 × 6 = 24   0 × 12 = 0
7 × 0 = 0   3 × 3 = 9   6 × 4 = 24   5 × 2 = 10   2 × 10 = 20
5 × 4 = 20   8 × 2 = 16   8 × 5 = 40   2 × 8 = 16   4 × 12 = 48
4 × 6 = 24   12 × 4 = 48 4 × 9 = 36   7 × 3 = 21   10 × 3 = 30
3 × 10 = 30   3 × 7 = 21   6 × 6 = 36   12 × 2 = 24 0 × 2 = 0
11 × 1 = 11   5 × 5 = 25   8 × 1 = 8   3 × 9 = 27   0 × 11 = 0
1 × 10 = 10   2 × 6 = 12   3 × 7 = 21   5 × 6 = 30   12 × 1 = 12

| Started: | Finished: | Total Time: | Completed: _____/80 | Correct: _____/80 |

Answers Up to 100

Name _____ Date _____

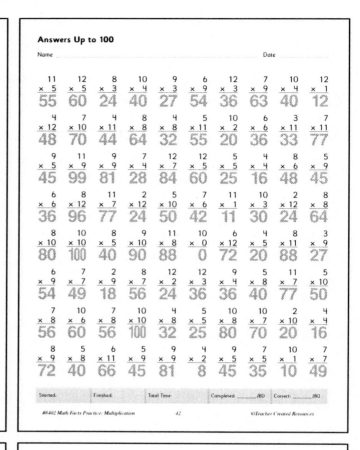

| Started: | Finished: | Total Time: | Completed: _____/80 | Correct: _____/80 |

Answers Across Up to 100

Name _____ Date _____

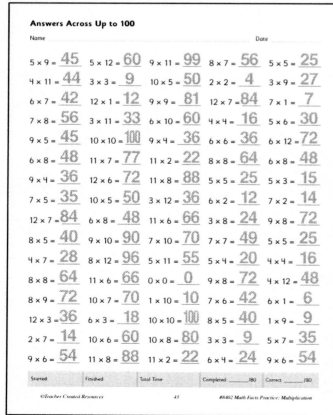

| Started: | Finished: | Total Time: | Completed: _____/80 | Correct: _____/80 |

Test #1

Name _____ Date _____

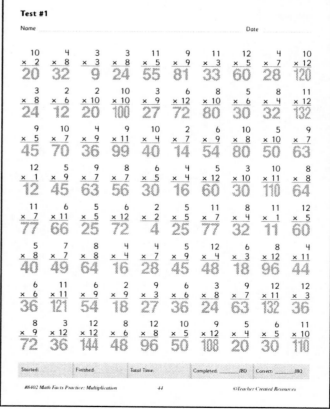

| Started: | Finished: | Total Time: | Completed: _____/80 | Correct: _____/80 |

Answer Keys (pages 45–48)

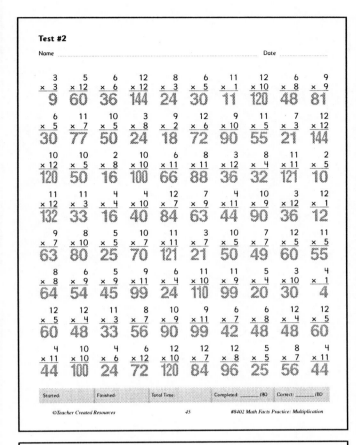

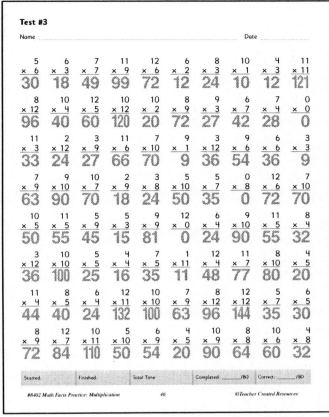

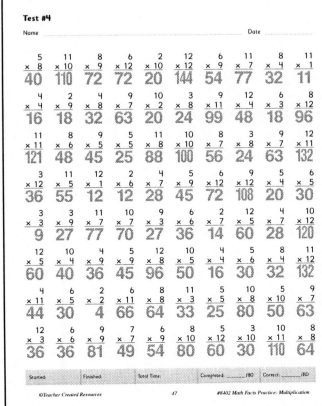

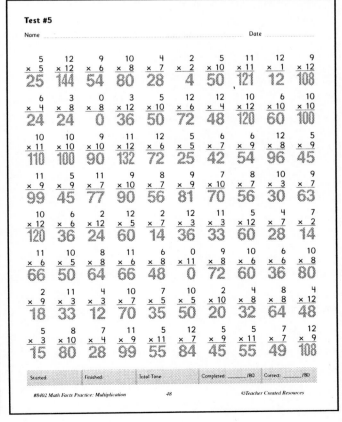

Answer Keys (pages 49–52)

Test #6

Name _____ Date _____

4 × 4 = 16	0 × 9 = 0	3 × 9 = 27	10 × 2 = 20	11 × 7 = 77
5 × 5 = 25	4 × 8 = 32	11 × 11 = 121	7 × 4 = 28	5 × 12 = 60
12 × 12 = 144	9 × 6 = 54	8 × 7 = 56	11 × 5 = 55	4 × 7 = 28
7 × 5 = 35	4 × 9 = 36	9 × 2 = 18	9 × 12 = 108	9 × 11 = 99
10 × 8 = 80	3 × 5 = 15	8 × 8 = 64	10 × 7 = 70	8 × 6 = 48
2 × 5 = 10	7 × 6 = 42	5 × 7 = 35	12 × 11 = 132	12 × 6 = 72
9 × 8 = 72	2 × 7 = 14	7 × 6 = 42	4 × 12 = 48	11 × 10 = 110
6 × 4 = 24	2 × 5 = 10	9 × 9 = 81	3 × 11 = 33	10 × 12 = 120
3 × 7 = 21	6 × 10 = 60	1 × 8 = 8	10 × 6 = 60	3 × 9 = 27
9 × 9 = 81	0 × 4 = 0	6 × 5 = 30	7 × 11 = 77	5 × 11 = 55
6 × 5 = 30	1 × 9 = 9	3 × 7 = 21	12 × 12 = 144	10 × 3 = 30
8 × 4 = 32	6 × 7 = 42	10 × 9 = 90	4 × 4 = 16	12 × 7 = 84
3 × 6 = 18	9 × 7 = 63	2 × 8 = 16	7 × 10 = 70	10 × 10 = 100
8 × 9 = 72	12 × 5 = 60	9 × 5 = 45	8 × 8 = 64	3 × 12 = 36
7 × 7 = 49	6 × 5 = 30	3 × 9 = 27	12 × 6 = 72	11 × 11 = 121
9 × 6 = 54	3 × 8 = 24	6 × 6 = 36	4 × 11 = 44	12 × 8 = 96

Started: _____ Finished: _____ Total Time: _____ Completed: _____/80 Correct: _____/80

Test #7

Name _____ Date _____

5 × 12 = 60	3 × 12 = 36	2 × 6 = 12	7 × 7 = 49	0 × 0 = 0
3 × 11 = 33	8 × 8 = 64	0 × 9 = 0	11 × 11 = 121	6 × 9 = 54
12 × 12 = 144	6 × 10 = 60	4 × 8 = 32	3 × 9 = 27	7 × 1 = 7
2 × 9 = 18	5 × 11 = 55	9 × 6 = 54	4 × 8 = 32	10 × 9 = 90
11 × 4 = 44	0 × 12 = 0	7 × 5 = 35	9 × 7 = 63	1 × 8 = 8
10 × 6 = 60	10 × 3 = 30	8 × 6 = 48	7 × 6 = 42	4 × 3 = 12
7 × 11 = 77	12 × 7 = 84	2 × 5 = 10	5 × 7 = 35	6 × 6 = 36
10 × 10 = 100	4 × 12 = 48	9 × 8 = 72	4 × 3 = 12	9 × 0 = 0
9 × 11 = 99	3 × 11 = 33	6 × 4 = 24	1 × 6 = 6	7 × 9 = 63
10 × 8 = 80	3 × 7 = 21	10 × 6 = 60	7 × 8 = 56	9 × 1 = 9
7 × 4 = 28	12 × 8 = 96	9 × 9 = 81	9 × 0 = 0	12 × 6 = 72
11 × 10 = 110	11 × 11 = 121	6 × 5 = 30	8 × 2 = 16	1 × 8 = 8
10 × 7 = 70	5 × 7 = 35	8 × 4 = 32	9 × 9 = 81	11 × 5 = 55
6 × 2 = 12	9 × 12 = 108	3 × 6 = 18	11 × 12 = 132	6 × 7 = 42
12 × 6 = 72	10 × 7 = 70	8 × 9 = 72	4 × 1 = 4	6 × 8 = 48
10 × 10 = 100	12 × 11 = 132	7 × 7 = 49	3 × 7 = 21	9 × 2 = 18

Started: _____ Finished: _____ Total Time: _____ Completed: _____/80 Correct: _____/80

Test #8

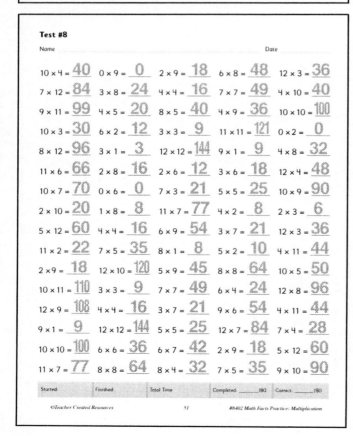

Name _____ Date _____

10 × 4 = 40	0 × 9 = 0	2 × 9 = 18	6 × 8 = 48	12 × 3 = 36
7 × 12 = 84	3 × 8 = 24	4 × 4 = 16	7 × 7 = 49	4 × 10 = 40
9 × 11 = 99	4 × 5 = 20	8 × 5 = 40	4 × 9 = 36	10 × 10 = 100
10 × 3 = 30	6 × 2 = 12	3 × 3 = 9	11 × 11 = 121	0 × 2 = 0
8 × 12 = 96	3 × 1 = 3	12 × 12 = 144	9 × 1 = 9	4 × 8 = 32
11 × 6 = 66	2 × 8 = 16	2 × 6 = 12	3 × 6 = 18	12 × 4 = 48
10 × 7 = 70	0 × 6 = 0	7 × 3 = 21	5 × 5 = 25	10 × 9 = 90
2 × 10 = 20	1 × 8 = 8	11 × 7 = 77	4 × 2 = 8	2 × 3 = 6
5 × 12 = 60	4 × 4 = 16	6 × 9 = 54	3 × 7 = 21	12 × 3 = 36
11 × 2 = 22	7 × 5 = 35	8 × 1 = 8	5 × 2 = 10	4 × 11 = 44
2 × 9 = 18	12 × 10 = 120	5 × 9 = 45	8 × 8 = 64	10 × 5 = 50
10 × 11 = 110	3 × 3 = 9	7 × 7 = 49	6 × 4 = 24	12 × 8 = 96
12 × 9 = 108	4 × 4 = 16	3 × 7 = 21	9 × 6 = 54	4 × 11 = 44
9 × 1 = 9	12 × 12 = 144	5 × 5 = 25	12 × 7 = 84	7 × 4 = 28
10 × 10 = 100	6 × 6 = 36	6 × 7 = 42	2 × 9 = 18	5 × 12 = 60
11 × 7 = 77	8 × 8 = 64	8 × 4 = 32	7 × 5 = 35	9 × 10 = 90

Started: _____ Finished: _____ Total Time: _____ Completed: _____/80 Correct: _____/80

Test #9

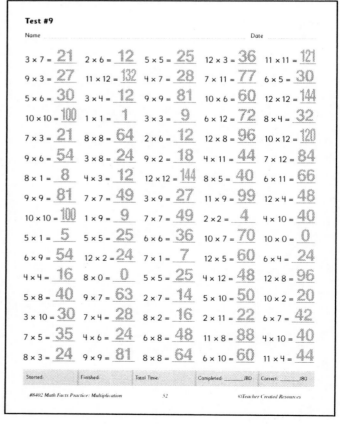

Name _____ Date _____

3 × 7 = 21	2 × 6 = 12	5 × 5 = 25	12 × 3 = 36	11 × 11 = 121
9 × 3 = 27	11 × 12 = 132	4 × 7 = 28	7 × 11 = 77	6 × 5 = 30
5 × 6 = 30	3 × 4 = 12	9 × 9 = 81	10 × 6 = 60	12 × 12 = 144
10 × 10 = 100	1 × 1 = 1	3 × 3 = 9	6 × 12 = 72	8 × 4 = 32
7 × 3 = 21	8 × 8 = 64	2 × 6 = 12	12 × 8 = 96	10 × 12 = 120
9 × 6 = 54	3 × 8 = 24	9 × 2 = 18	4 × 11 = 44	7 × 12 = 84
8 × 1 = 8	4 × 3 = 12	12 × 12 = 144	8 × 5 = 40	6 × 11 = 66
9 × 9 = 81	7 × 7 = 49	3 × 9 = 27	11 × 9 = 99	12 × 4 = 48
10 × 10 = 100	1 × 9 = 9	7 × 7 = 49	2 × 2 = 4	4 × 10 = 40
5 × 1 = 5	5 × 5 = 25	6 × 6 = 36	10 × 7 = 70	10 × 0 = 0
6 × 9 = 54	12 × 2 = 24	7 × 1 = 7	12 × 5 = 60	6 × 4 = 24
4 × 4 = 16	8 × 0 = 0	5 × 5 = 25	4 × 12 = 48	12 × 8 = 96
5 × 4 = 40	9 × 7 = 63	2 × 7 = 14	5 × 10 = 50	10 × 2 = 20
3 × 10 = 30	7 × 4 = 28	8 × 2 = 16	2 × 11 = 22	6 × 7 = 42
7 × 5 = 35	4 × 6 = 24	6 × 8 = 48	11 × 8 = 88	4 × 10 = 40
8 × 3 = 24	9 × 9 = 81	8 × 8 = 64	6 × 10 = 60	11 × 4 = 44

Started: _____ Finished: _____ Total Time: _____ Completed: _____/80 Correct: _____/80